The Art of Play

An Adult's Guide to Reclaiming Imagination and Spontaneity

Adam Blatner, M.D.

University of Louisville School of Medicine
Louisville, Kentucky

Allee Blatner

HUMAN SCIENCES PRESS, INC.
72 FIFTH AVENUE
NEW YORK, N.Y. 10011-8004

To the many people who participated in our Art of Play sessions, especially our friends in Santa Rosa, California. Their willingness to engage in spontaneous enactments helped us refine the method and showed us how wonderful it is when adults engage in imaginative play together.

Copyright © 1988 by Human Sciences Press, Inc.
72 Fifth Avenue, New York, New York 10011

Printed in the United States of America
987654321

Library of Congress Cataloging-in-Publication Data

Blatner, Adam.
  The art of play.

  Bibliography: p.
  Includes index.
  1. Play—Psychological aspects. 2. Role playing—Therapeutic use.
I. Blatner, Allee. II. Title.
BF717.B57 1987   302.3′4   86-27419
ISBN 0-89885-355-9
      0-89885-359-1 (pbk.)

CONTENTS

NOTE TO READERS

Because of the awkwardness inherent in constructing sentences so as to avoid sexist language, the author has chosen to use the generic "he" at those times when "one" or "they" would have been cumbersome.

FOREWORD

The Art of Play is an important book for many reasons. First and foremost is the fact that it really accomplishes what it sets out to do, namely to lead the reader into the *practice,* that is, the *art* of play. It is, indeed, the prime book to teach the adult the practice of play. While there have been many works on almost every aspect of play, it is strange that there have been few that have recognized the necessity of play. While it has been recognized that all mammals when young are characterized by an impulse to play, there has, in the Western World, been a failure to recognize that the need to play remains a necessity throughout one's life, a biosocial necessity. The four great chords of mental health are the ability to love, to work, to play, and to think soundly. It is remarkable how closely interwoven each of these abilities is with one another. How is love related to work, and love and work related to play, and to thinking soundly? Does the scientist, whether in the laboratory or his study, love what he is doing that other people call work? Indeed, it is work, but it is also play, a loving drudgery at times, but still loving and play, and great fun, even though on occasion it may involve

7

a great deal of frustration. But what are frustrations for, if not to be overcome? What is a life without stress and strain—without anxiety? The answer is that there is no such life; that these are conditions which are necessary challenges requiring equally necessary responses. It is the great merit of Dr. and Mrs. Blatner's book that through their considerable experience in practically helping others to learn how to meet the challenges of life through play, they have done so in so effective a manner.

Ashley Montagu, Ph.D.

INTRODUCTION

"Come and play." Remember the warmth and magic of those words? They were an invitation to happy times spent with playmates; you entered a special realm of make-believe. There, you were super-heroes or monsters, mommies or babies, animals, explorers, airplanes, explosions. You could be anything your imagination could conjure. How intimate and personal such activities were for you. And yet, those roles were impersonal too, in the sense that they expressed dimensions other than the familiar concerns of your everyday life; thus, the pleasurable pastime of role-playing provided a pleasant distancing from more self-conscious experiences.

Though this activity was very much a part of your natural heritage, it may have become increasingly neglected as you grew older. Many people seem to believe that spontaneous play must remain a part of childhood. The essential elements of this powerful facet of human nature cannot be repressed, however, and will continue to be exercised in adult life in various ways. In our culture its expression tends to get focused on the relatively constricting structures of competitive and performance-oriented games and arts. The Art of Play offers a way to reclaim the original channel of your vitality by allowing play to become a vehicle for the enhancement of your creativity and social involvement.

The activity of make-believe play usually includes enacting roles with others, and the Art of Play is an extension of informal, improvisational dramatics, adapted for a group of adults. It is an especially rewarding and important form of playfulness that can be a potential source of pleasurable recreation—aesthetically, personally, and socially.

The purpose of this book is to offer you both practical techniques and an intellectual framework for experimenting with imaginative drama as an art form or mode of recreation. The Art of Play is to be enjoyed simply for the experience itself, for interacting with others in a socially pleasant context, and for discovering what it feels like in different roles. It's a vehicle that allows for the integration of the playful use of other expressive art forms, such as singing, dancing, drawing, or the use of costume. It is not done for the purposes of performing for an audience or for competition.

"The Art of Play" refers to both an attitude and practice in everyday life as well as being a term to describe a specific method for working with a group of adults. In the first case, we are proposing that infusing our adult lives with elements of spontaneity is a valuable and healthful activity. Throughout this book will be found ideas that will help you connect ways you can do it for yourself and those you care about. The second use of the term names the specific group experience that we have developed to guide adults on an exploration of channels to their own imagery and spontaneity. This group method will be presented in greater detail in Chapters 4 and 5.

The Plan of This Book

We begin with an exploration of the psychological nature of playfulness and its benefits, followed by a presentation of the method of the Art of Play as one way to enjoy these benefits. After detailing an example of how the method can be used in extended enactments, we then offer approaches to building the basic skills for the exercise of this form. The cultural factors that have inhibited the fullest enjoyment of playfulness in our culture are reviewed, preparatory to a discussion of applications of the principles and techniques inherent in the Art of Play in education, psychotherapy, and other contexts. We finish with some general and philosophical considerations, followed by a wealth of references for further study.

The Background of This Approach

The Art of Play is an adaptation of sociodrama. The make-believe play of young children which involves others in an enactment of various social situations has come to be called "sociodramatic play" by many scientists in the field of child development. We shall at times refer to the main approach of this book by that term, or, for variety, use generally equivalent terms such as "creative drama," "improvisatory enactment," or "imaginative role-playing." Sociodrama is a modification of a method of group psychotherapy called psychodrama. Jacob L. Moreno, M.D. originated the method in the early 1920s in Vienna.[1] Instead of talking *about* their hopes, dreams, and conflicts, Moreno had his patients *show* the feelings and situations to the therapists and patients in the group setting. Psychodrama is a very powerful psychotherapeutic approach, and it has many applications.

In psychodrama, the focus is on the individual, and the individual's unique combination of role conflicts existing in real life. In sociodrama, however, group members explore the conflicts inherent in general role relationships, such as mothers and daughters, policemen and delinquent teenagers, teachers and students, or between people of different ethnic or racial backgrounds. Anyone in the group can play the key roles in an enactment, and often the group facilitator uses psychodramatic techniques such as role reversal, asides, or future-projection in order to bring out more feelings and help the participants understand each other on a more vivid and authentic basis.

The well-known technique of "role-playing" is a direct

offshoot of Moreno's psychodramatic method; originally it referred to enactments that tended to be practice sessions for working out better approaches to awkward interpersonal situations. Later, the term became roughly interchangeable with psychodrama and sociodrama. When children enact general roles in a context of spontaneous recreation, such as playing house, being animals in a forest, etc., this activity is called "sociodramatic play," a natural form of sociodrama.

As a psychiatrist with over 20 years of clinical experience, I find psychodrama and sociodrama to be valuable additions to the array of concepts and methods I call upon in the course of working with patients. Over the years I have become impressed with two major issues. First, one component of psychotherapy is a kind of learning; much of this can be taught as part of the curricula of high schools, colleges, and continuing education programs. In other words, I see the need for *preventive* approaches in the maintenance of mental health.

The second insight comes from my many experiences using psychodramatic methods as part of helping people clarify problems or open their imaginations. The very act of creating roles has potential beyond the actual content of the problem being addressed. Simply taking roles, developing and varying them, then shifting to other roles, vitalizes the individual. By using the exercise of role reversal to expand beyond constricted habits of looking at the world from only one point of view, patients begin to think about how others might feel in relationship to them.

Most importantly, I have discovered that patients find role-playing and psychodrama to be challenging, interesting, and fun. My use of these methods shifts the mood of individual, family, or group therapy sessions to something more playful. The people involved start interacting on a different level, more as equals. They are more equal because their official roles are subordinated to the process of creative enactment, in which everyone can generate original and enjoyable ideas. In this realm new approaches and solutions to personal and interpersonal difficulties can emerge.

Allee Blatner, the coauthor of this book, has a longstanding interest in extending opportunities for creative expression to more people. Her own academic training and experience in the arts made her aware of the resources available for anyone's use. She sensed that, in the right context, adults could freely blend drawing, characterizations, movement, and singing to explore and enjoy the richness of their mature imaginations.

The foundation for adult play clearly emerged when we eliminated performance (for oneself or others), rejoined audience and performer in their natural sociodramatic play state, and envisioned a medium dedicated solely to individual and collective creative, imaginative exploration. The significance of our concerns united in the acknowledgment that there is no channel for adults to play this way. We have created a context and social activity where such play can be experienced. It is a synthesis of psychodramatic methods being used in the service of enactments of characters and situations arising out of group members' imaginations.

The Stage Is Enough

Children naturally play in a sociodramatic fashion. Adults are somewhat envious of children in their ability to pretend and relate innocently to the magic realm of make-believe. Many adults have preserved some of their role-playing inclinations. It is difficult, however, to get social validation for such behavior, aside from occasional costume parties. The opportunity to create characters has been relegated to the rigorous and competitive world of professional acting, and most people have neither the energy nor the talent for such a dedicated pursuit. So, the populace as a whole has had to be satisfied with being spectators.

Sociodramatic play has many of the advantages of therapeutic sociodrama, but without the requirement of the participants having a "problem." This frees it to be a kind of recreation, socialization, experimentation, and even an art form. The activity of creating and playing with dramatic roles can be refined; the source of childlike natural play can thereby be cultivated into a mature, flexible, highly conscious group of skills.

Several years ago, we began working with groups of

friends, and they got right into it! It became apparent that, as Moreno said, "the stage is enough." The first groups of people demonstrated from the beginning that they could play with the innocence of their childhood *and* the sophistication of their accumulated experience as adults. The participants generally had great fun and played in ways they thought they'd almost forgotten.

Our basic approach for a successful adult play group includes the following issues:

> Give people the opportunity to create characters based on ideas that spontaneously come out of their imaginations.
>
> Create a warm, supportive context where this behavior is the only game that's being played.
>
> Keep the group small enough so everyone can play, and it is not alienating (about nine people).
>
> Set aside sufficient time to let people get involved and to wind down afterwards (at least 2 to 3 hours).
>
> Continually eliminate all judgment, competitiveness, and psychologizing.
>
> Have someone maintain a flow of activities, and play the role of director or facilitator.

As we have refined the method, cultural, philosophical, historical, psychological, and practical implications have become apparent. These will be described in the next several chapters.

The Art of Play in Perspective

This book focuses on the applications of **imaginative, pretend play** as a vehicle for adult recreation and artistic expression. As such, it is a complement to several other movements in our culture:

> "New Games"
> Improvisational Theater

Creative Dramatics, Educational Dramatics
Drama Therapy

The field of New Games was developed by Stewart Brand and Pat Farrington, among others, in the early 1970s. It has been followed by a variety of other programs and books that describe and discuss a range of noncompetitive games.[2,3,4]

The movement toward improvisational theater has grown significantly in the last generation. Stimulated by the work of Konstantin Stanislavsky, Viola Spolin, and others, "Improv" is a form that revitalizes the theater by cultivating elements of spontaneity.[5,6]

Creative and Educational Dramatics are important movements for fostering the many benefits of play as part of the school experience of teaching and learning. A rigorous commitment to how learning can best be facilitated is greatly aided by integrating these approaches.[7] It is exciting to note the growing number of school boards that are including creative dramatics activities as part of their essential elements of teaching.

Drama Therapy has changed radically since around 1970, and thereby it has evolved into a much more dynamic approach. Previously, it involved patients putting on short scripted and rehearsed plays; but now there is an emphasis on improvisational activities that can broaden the patients' role repertoires.[8]

The Art of Play is a method that complements and integrates aspects of these other approaches. It emphasizes spontaneous dramatic enactment, with a spirit similar to that of New Games. While it is improvisational, there is no concern for performing for an audience. The focus, rather, is simply on creating and experiencing the roles being played. It is similar to Creative Dramatics, but it is aimed at adults and older teenagers; in addition, it uses certain techniques to deepen the exploration of the characters and their situations. Drawing on similarities with Drama Therapy, it moves outside the treatment of problems, and extends the resources of healing and growth to applications in social, artistic, recreational, and other settings.

The heart of our method lies in its philosophical commitment to noncompetition. This is then made real for the participants through the environment of play which the group leaders establish and maintain. The attitude of the director/facilitator is more important than clever techniques or exciting experiences. The quality of the time spent in a session is the final gauge of the success of a group. More about the director's role is found in Chapter 4.

Because the Art of Play is a useful tool with ample flexibility, its methods and activities can also be applied in the fields of therapy, education, and theatrical training. Thus, readers with interest in these and other areas will find a wealth of compatible ideas in the following chapters.

Can Make-Believe Play Be an "Art"?

When we named our approach "The Art of Play," we had a number of relevant associations in mind. Activities can be considered artistic or art forms in many ways. There are articles or books with titles like *The Art of Cooking*, *The Art of Gardening*, or *The Art of Sailing*. In this sense, "art" refers to engaging in ordinary roles in a way that integrates aesthetic enrichment, mindfulness, and a continual process of refinement. The use of the word "art" also refers to activities in which there is a flow of inspiration or imagery into a process, filling it with spontaneity and creativity. Sometimes this frame of reference differentiates unique and original explorations from repetitive crafts. "Art" is applied in a third way to activities that reflect a high degree of skill, refinement, sensitivity, and discipline.

Another way of thinking about this is that there is an "art" involved in bringing forth the creativity in others. Indeed, such a discipline could become an art form in itself, allied with a kind of teaching of the creative and expressive arts that would emphasize the developing imagination and spontaneity in students rather than perfecting products. Refocusing on the importance of the process of each individual could be part of a trend toward integrating more archetypally feminine values into education and culture.

Learning the Basic Skills

An audience of adults who wish to engage in make-believe play require more than verbal encouragement about the benefits of playfulness; there must also be a *way* to learn and organize the component activities. We have solved this through a gradual series of exercises such as those used by students of drama or psychodrama. Some practical guidelines are offered in Chapters 6 through 9. As you read the material, you will be reminded of parts of yourself you haven't really forgotten—the way your "inner child" still knows how to play. As you reenter this process consciously as an adult, you'll discover the component skills are often the very *opposite* of the habits of thinking and acting you have developed in the course of most educational training. Most of us have become habituated to focusing attention on a search for a correct answer. Instead of being objective and rational, you may often need to remind yourself to allow subjective and emotional ideas to come to mind. In addition, effort has no value and needs to be set aside in order for you to rediscover your capacity to enter a natural flow of images and interactions. Cultivating imaginative playfulness benefits from and requires a free-floating attention that is sensitive to your intuition and aesthetically exciting ideas.

Spontaneous play is somewhat like swimming, driving a car, or riding a bicycle. It entails a skill you acquire by personally doing and experiencing the process. Books and lectures are clearly limited as ways of learning these activities. Also, as mentioned earlier, learning to play requires a realignment of your mental orientation and this may challenge old habits. Just as balancing on a bicycle involves a new way of relating to gravity in an unfamiliar medium, the old sources of security are shifted, your stability is maintained by the new activity of continuing your motion rather than by holding still; likewise, improvisatory play also requires continued involvement when faced with novelty, and it requires your willingness to accept an element of risk. Much of this will become familiar to you as you begin to play again, just as once you've ever learned to swim you don't completely forget it. In a group setting that is nonjudgmental, supportive, and with someone who can serve as a guide, director, or facilitator, the process of relearning imaginative enactment can be made enjoyable. This book will offer an intellectual framework and suggest a variety of techniques; however, the real skill-building can only evolve through your practice.

A New Field

The Art of Play is a contribution to a recent emergence of Play as a field unto itself. In addition to the four areas of specialization mentioned earlier, the investigation of play is included in anthropology, child development, psychology, physical education, ethology, theology, and a growing number of other disciplines. The study and exercise of playfulness is part of what seems to be a trend in our culture toward reviving and reinstating the place of the socially inclusive, "right-brained" dimensions of human activity.

You are exploring a new frontier, and as you experiment with your own interpretations and modifications of the material we present in this book, we'd like to hear about your ideas, experiences, and suggestions. The theme of the Art of Play is an invitation to you to reclaim your innate spontaneity and imagination from the nostalgic realm of happy childhood memories, and to integrate these vitalizing dimensions into your adult life. Our hope is that you will develop the component skills well enough to initiate creative play activities in your everyday lives for the purposes of learning, sharing, exploring, and just plain fun. In the spirit of a Chinese proverb, we offer these methods as an alternative to the pervasive spectator/audience role in our culture:

> If you give a man a fish, you feed him for a day.
> If you teach a man to fish, you feed him for the rest of his life.

Chapter 1

A PSYCHOLOGY AND PHILOSOPHY OF PLAY

The value of imaginative, sociodramatic play may be understood more fully in the context of the union of a holistic, integrative psychology with a philosophy that focuses on the creative process as a central element. The connecting link between the two is the phenomenon of spontaneity, that particular quality of mind in nature which allows for novelty and creativity to emerge.

Role Dynamics

We have formulated a psychology which addresses the importance of such phenomena as excitement, playfulness, celebration, delight, and enjoyment through creativity. Even though noted by other theories, we believe these phenomena need to be recognized as vital channels of motivation, self-expression, socialization, and skill building. Because of their significance, they deserve to be explored in depth. We have given the name **role dynamics** to this method which synthesizes a number of other types of psychology—humanistic, existential, analytic, developmental, transpersonal, social, etc.

Rather than seeking its unifying principle in the realm of motivations, role dynamics acknowledges the sheer variety of human needs. Indeed, it makes the multidimensionality of human experience its central premise: People play a multiplicity of roles in their lives, and by understanding and becoming creative with these roles, we can learn to make our lives richer and more effective. In role dynamics we focus particular attention on an appreciation of human nature as a deeply *social* phenomenon.

Healthy development in our psychology is viewed as a process of role expansion in many dimensions. For example, our approach adds several more social phases of early childhood development which correspond to and, in most cases, are more relevant than the traditional analytic psychosexual oral, anal, phallic, and oedipal stages. We propose the "dermal," "playful," "useful," and "cooperative" stages, respectively. These processes accommodate a more interpersonal and collective viewpoint. In addition, they offer a balancing alternative to what we feel has become a bias towards individualism in much of psychology.[1] Most importantly, role dynamics utilizes the healthiest experiences as the norm for assessing development. This is in contrast to the more limited descriptions made by psychoanalytic theories of child development. Moreover, our stages of development remain relevant for healthy functioning and extend throughout the life of the person by continuing to define significant areas that need to be cared for at age ninety, as well as at nine or nineteen years.

The dermal phase in role dynamics refers to the importance of skin contacts, as well as the sensations of pressure, balance, heat, etc. The skin is the largest organ in the human body, and as the experiments of the Harlows with the baby monkeys in the 1960s demonstrated, physical contact is more important than mere feeding. Being held, cuddled, caressed, rocked, and other sensual experiences are essential for healthy psychological development. Moreover, in comparison to the oral experience of feeding, the skin offers as rich (if not richer) a source of pleasurable social bonding, sensuality, and discovery. Looking at child development from this perspective acknowledges the significant role of fathers, older siblings, and other members of the intimate community in healthy maturation.

The next phase, the playful, overlaps with and emerges out of the dermal, occupying around the fifth to the twenty-fourth month and beyond. Infants then begin to integrate their own initiative with the richness of human relationships. In the healthiest forms of this phase, there are many opportunities for mutual adventures, balanced experiences of activity and receptivity on both sides, introduction of novelty and allowance of time for assimilation, variations of pacing and intensity.[2] Sensitivity, time, and empathy are required on the part of the parent, and these pleasant interactions for the infant become the basis for a deep reservoir of pleasure and positive expectations, which in turn give the child strength in dealing with the inevitable frustrations of the coming years. Moreover, play extends the role repertoire to include explorations of song, funny faces, wordplay, and other modes of aesthetic, not directly utilitarian, behavior.

The playful phase corresponds to and reframes the implicit struggle so often associated with the anal stage in analytic theory. From the individualistic focus of a training metaphor in which children must learn to frustrate and control themselves, our playful phase represents the opportunity for cooperative socialization. By using an age-specific game that goes beyond the physical issue, it introduces to the growing child the idea that there are places for things: for shoes and books and poops and pee. The child can enjoy the mastery in learning to put things where they belong.

Building upon a healthy playful foundation, the next phases continue to emphasize agreeable socialization rather than individualistic dominance. Extending the play of putting things in the right place, the child becomes aware of participation with people and what people do. Helping feed the pets, clean the table, or sweep the driveway can become enjoyable games that include the feeling of helping, of experiencing being appreciated and thanked. The analytic phallic "Look at me" is incorporated into our "useful" phase and would be stated in a more social context as "How can I help?"

Ample opportunities still exist in this schema to validate

individuality, in the sense of being recognized for one's originality or special blend of strengths and weaknesses. It is important to differentiate this from an overemphasis on individualism, in which the boundary of mutuality is broken and a person expects or gets special recognition and privileges even at another's expense. We propose the use of collective play experiences to heighten the healthy elements of self-esteem without promoting subtle pathological narcissism.

The next step, extending further the natural cognitive maturation and socialization process, corresponds to the analytic oedipal stage. Between four and six, children begin to learn to play with more than one other person at a time. The challenge involves joining a small group without being caught up in alliances. The interpersonal dynamic is often much more significant than the intrapsychic experiences involving sexual imagery. This cooperative stage can develop quite smoothly in situations where the previous experiences have been satisfying and the group (or parents) are themselves friendly and inclusive.

For instance, when Adam's son, David, was five, he addressed this stage while the two of them were alone together by announcing to Adam, "I'm going to marry Mommy." Adam answered with mild curiosity and friendliness, "But what about me? I'm already married to Mommy." David thought for a moment, then made a simple synthesis: "Well, I'll marry you, too." Both of them started laughing, the laughter also reflecting David's partial yet implicit knowledge that one can't marry more than one person at a time. As shall be discussed in the next chapter, the playful capacity to celebrate paradox allows for a symbolic yet satisfactory solution to many problems.

There is much more to the psychology of role dynamics; in fact, we are writing a book about it. The point is, we believe this psychology which views human nature as being essentially collective, as well as individual, is an important tool in learning to think in terms of how we can contribute to preventing or resolving a number of our contemporary personal and societal problems. Another advantage to the role concept as a basis for a modern psychology is its implicit invitation to become creative and flexible with the roles we use in your lives. A great deal of healthy functioning can be developed through practice in responsibly shifting roles. Play's natural expansion of the range of roles we have available serves to broaden and lubricate the process of human interaction.

Spontaneity

One of the pivotal concepts in relation to play is that of spontaneity. This is rather hard to define, and is elusive because it involves the process of transcending structure itself—the process of questioning definitions and making redefinitions. In that way, it participates in the paradoxical nature of play as described in the following chapter.

If you find yourself wondering if you're spontaneous enough to explore improvisational playfulness, be assured that (a) the principles in this book are designed so that you need not feel self-conscious, (b) you'll discover that you've got more access to spontaneity than you might have thought, and (c) your ability to channel spontaneity will develop with practice, just as in other areas requiring cultivation of skills. Everyone has some experience with spontaneity, and it varies in each role and activity. You can learn to expand the function of this process in your life.

Spontaneity involves a quality of mind, the active opening up which accompanies the thinking of a new idea or trying something a new way. It involves thinking afresh, balancing impulse and restraint, and integrating imagination, reason, and intuition. Spontaneity is the process by which inspiration enters creativity. *It is more than mere impulsivity* because it requires some *intention* to achieve an aesthetic or constructive effect.

Spontaneity also may be understood as the *opposite* of habit, stereotyped thinking, neurotic compulsive rituals, or transferences (interpersonal patterns that mimic earlier experiences, rather than interacting with people and events in the here and now). In being spontaneous, you are open to how the present moment is different from the past, and how the people around you might be able to offer new and more rewarding experiences.[3]

Obviously, and yet worth mentioning, spontaneity is fun. You may discover, however, as you begin to explore sociodramatic play, that you experience some vague anxieties, guilts, or other subtle discomforts. This may be part of what many people have learned about distrusting the pursuit of pleasure. Enjoying pleasure is often partially repressed and somewhat disreputable in our culture. Some of the reasons for this are noted in Chapters 10 through 12 and deserve to be thought about when you decide to begin exploring imaginative play. When things are repressed, they remain undifferentiated. For example, the difference between wholesome and unwholesome fun is not often discussed. Our culture tends to foster confusion by overexaggerating emotions and flooding us with images of sex/eroticism and power/aggression. (Although the entertainment business claims to be responding to the tastes of the free market, many commentators on our culture are now proposing that the tastes for primitive and intense symbolic experiences are actually being created in order to sell a product. The success of junk food has been achieved through expensive advertising and promotional propaganda, and the electronic and graphics industries appear to be actively using similar methods.)

The idea of fun is further complicated by getting associated with irresponsible frivolity, destructive behaviors, or self-indulgent hedonism. These are actually maladaptive forms of enjoyment and are characterized by feelings of pent-up anger, worthlessness, and rebellion, often in response to oppressive or coercive situations. They are seen in the behaviors of those adolescents who cannot find enjoyable and meaningful involvements in their (compulsory) school, and have joined the epidemic of drug and alcohol abuse.[4] Thus, when they have time off, or when they drop out, they engage in drug-related short-term attempts at having "fun" which in the long run result in a vacuous boredom.

Therefore, in the presence of all these negative associations, we need to remind ourselves of the large array of deeply enjoyable pleasures to choose from. Activities that are richer in resources, more sustainable, more responsible, and often more social include: the arts, storytelling, having adventures, being useful in creating celebrations, exploring/contemplating nature and spiritual experiences, trying out the full range of sports and games, and informal role-playing activities such as the Art of Play.

Having acknowledged potential obstacles resulting from your own psychosocial inhibitions to play, let's remember that it is fun. Indeed, that may be the simplest definition of play. You can celebrate with delight the discoveries of new potentialities arising out of your unconscious, the magic of allowing the inspiration of the Muses to act through you, the joy of surprise with the events that occur in a receptive, co-creative state of mind, and the deep sense of belonging that occurs when you and others share the intimacy of bringing forth each other's images. Spontaneity then becomes a value as well as a psychological phenomenon and, as such, deserves consideration from a philosophical point of view.

Having Fun—A Philosophical Reflection

A modern tradition in philosophy addresses itself to the implications of the possibilities of evolution and the discoveries of modern science. We refer, especially, to the writings of such philosophers as Alfred North Whitehead, Charles Hartshorne, Pierre Teilhard de Chardin, and Ken Wilber,[5-8] among others. What these thinkers share is a view of the universe as an essentially creative process. Our human role in this universe is something similar to the cells in the brain of an evolving, cosmic embryo. As humans learn to relate to each other more harmoniously, it is as if we all are participating in a great process of awakening.

Not only are our responsible acts of co-creation included in this process, but also our experiences of learning and enjoyment. This philosophical view is partly based on the validity of the aesthetic component in events both great and small.[9] Another way of saying this is that having fun may be a potentially important part of the way everything operates in the universe.

In order to explore this concept, we invite you to consider the following intuitive exposition, one which may be the way things are:

To begin, let us imagine that pleasure pervades the universe—every action involves at least a rudimentary experiential reaction. Whitehead has applied this even on the atomic level, but we'll focus our illustrations on the realms of those events that involve the generally recognized forms of life. For example, the cricket's "singing" may be a deliciously sensual experience for the creature as it rubs its special appendages together. The one-celled animals in the ocean may be savoring the taste of their food during the milliseconds of their ingesting process. And the even more minute creatures from which they choose, the algae and bacteria, may be enjoying the sun's warmth as the radiation catalyzes their various internal chemical processes.

Purely rational, dry "explanations" of animal behavior shouldn't prevent us from contemplating the possible feelings generated in the course of something being alive. This is not meant to imply animals experience pleasure in the same way humans do, as commonly seen in the anthropomorphic characters in children's stories. Nonetheless it seems presumptuous for us to claim that they don't experience anything, considering the complexity of their behavior. Indeed, we suspect that in some ways human experiences and consciousness are a wonderful complexification of a spectrum of inherent feelings in all life.

If hunger and fear "motivate" certain behaviors, then consider the likelihood of feelings, however brief, when a creature catches its prey, or takes the first bite, or, on the other hand, senses that it has successfully evaded and escaped its potential predator. There is probably a gradient of feeling, a sense of greater dissatisfaction, leading to behavior, leading to a sense of relative satisfaction or pleasure even in the most rudimentary functions of excreting, discovering a richer, more oxygenated environment, or shifting from rest to activity or back again.

The mystery of sex and parenting involves subtle components that deserve contemplation. Beyond the culmination of orgasm, the mating behavior of most animals involves discrimination, preference, and choosing some experiences over others because they appear to offer more fun to the participants. Attraction, courting, nest building, the rearing of offspring, all are enormously complex phenomena which also undoubtedly involve pleasure. Other examples include the singing of many species of birds, the strategies and chasing behaviors of some predators, and the building of insect colonies.

A study of biology from the point of view of considering the personal experience of the living creatures themselves can lead to a vivid sense of the aesthetic dimensions pervading existence. In turn, it suggests that the motivation of children and adults toward pleasure is a natural phenomenon. Based on a holistic perspective, the philosophical implications of a universe which has vivid experiences invites the integration of fun as an important *value*. Recognizing and honoring fun from these perspectives sets the tone for the rest of our book.

Chapter 2

THE PLEASURES OF PARADOX

Further Reflections on the Psychology of Play

One of the most obvious things about people is that they play; yet this is rarely addressed in any depth in most standard psychology texts. A good deal of what we call culture is based on playful activities, since these embody exploratory and celebrational experience.[1]

Playfulness is the theme of this book, and particularly that point in play when the imagination and spontaneity begin to add some degree of elaboration, style, and originality. Play differs from work in being an activity done for its own sake, for fun. Play is also the major activity of the child; it is engaged in seriously by children.[2] There are forms of play that may be relaxing, enjoyable, exploratory, and yet aren't playful because the activity has not yet reached a stage where there is enough mastery for it to be spontaneous. For example, in learning to swim or ride a bicycle, the actual learning of the skill could be considered a form of play; then there's a point when you go on to discover new techniques that for you seem original, such as developing new styles of splashing the water in interesting patterns or riding "no hands." At that point play becomes playfulness.

There are many different expressions in which playfulness can occur and here are a few to warm you up to thinking about this area:

singing	building	storytelling
toys	exploring	conversing
drawing	ceremonies	games
leaping	sliding	sports
swinging	wordplay	rolling
watching	climbing	jokes[3]

A number of theories exist regarding the nature and function of play in child development and animal behavior. We think the most useful is a synthesis of depth psychology and the communication theories of play, as described by Gregory Bateson. This will be presented more fully in the following pages.

Play as Paradox

The make-believe play of childhood and the dramatic mode both reflect the same psychological process, the ability of the mind to create a special category of experience called playfulness. This is a condition of social interaction in which behavior doesn't carry the same meaning as it might in the "ordinary" or nonplay set of experience. The phenomenon of play thus involves a paradox, a condition in which something is both real and not real at the same time. The mind seems to experience a kind of pleasure in being able to encompass these seemingly irreconcilable opposites; it's a form of mental juggling. There is a kind of mastery, aesthetic tension, cathartic release, humorous amusement, and, in short, delight in discovering the subtle cleverness of mentally manipulating perceptions and cognitions. This pleasure is increased when it can be shared with others.

The late Gregory Bateson, noted anthropologist and communications theorist, described this paradoxical nature of play, particularly as a special type of communication. This idea relates to contemporary theories of systems and differing logical types. There are practical implications in an approach to experience that acknowledges that humans think and relate to each other on many different levels at the same time. The most exciting of these for our purposes is the illumination of the process of play as an activity that includes more than one level of meaning, and the enjoyment that results from shifting between these levels.[4]

We want to add to this the idea that there might be a primary motivation and expression of what Freud called "the pleasure principle" in play itself, the experience of overcoming apparent paradox. It seems the mind finds pleasure in manipulating its own inconsistencies—the process gives some mastery over confusion, allows the imagination to expand, and extends the sense of identity to include a greater range of experience.[5] In other words, it's fun to juggle incongruous perceptions in the mind—to joke and go on roller coasters and to pretend.

For instance, the early games of infancy such as peekaboo have a psychoanalytic explanation that involves the baby's learning to control its anxiety regarding separations from the mother by developing a rudimentary intellectual capacity for knowing that something is still there, even when it cannot be directly seen—which is called "object constancy." We would emphasize yet another dynamic—the enjoyment of paradox itself. The growing child delights in feeling the subtle tension between perceiving something as being there and not being there at the same time. This is an act of internal balancing, the play of paradox. Later on, much of what is considered play or humor contains this element of internal incongruity. An example of this is an object or role in one category, such as an important, dignified, authority figure, who suddenly shifts into another logically inconsistent category, such as appearing ridiculous as he gets a cream pie thrown in his face.[6]

The Magic Power of "If"

A key word that functions as a signal for the change of definition of the reality-status of a proposition is the word "if." Sometimes this word is implied rather than explicitly stated. A special grammatical form called the "subjunctive" tense occurs in many languages. It is used in the case of events that exist conditionally, or as possibilities, rather than actualities. For example, "I would go with you **if** we could get a baby-sitter," or "I might like this" (here, the "if" is implied). "I wish I could do that." "**If** I were you I wouldn't do that." The subjunctive tense, with its use of distancing words like "would," "might," or "were," is similar in general function to the playful context.[7]

In play, participants make an implicit agreement: "Now we will behave **as if** our roles and interactions are real, while at the same time knowing that they are not 'really real' in the sense of having the ordinary requirements and consequences of everyday life." This is accomplished through a set of verbal and nonverbal signals indicating that the subsequent behavior should be understood as play. Metacommunications is the term to describe messages that modify the meaning of the obvious content.

The old movie cliché, "Smile when you say that, pardner," is an example of how a metacommunication can change the significance of a statement. In other words, if you smile, a remark ordinarily provoking retaliation won't be acted upon and, furthermore, it will be an acknowledgment of the other's power. Instead of spelling out all these interpersonal negotiations in cumbersome verbal agreements, a simple gesture, facial expression, tone of voice or inflection, the directionality of eye contact, or the chosen context, all serve as metacommunications that modify the meaning of whatever is said. Most direct interactions among humans and animals involve many levels of communication all occurring in simultaneous and interpenetrating complexes. These shifts of rhythm and action can be very quick and subtle, happening within the timespan of tenths of a second. Through such cues and reactions bear cubs can engage freely in rough-and-tumble mock combat without hurting each other.

Since psychological and social processes exist in a network of multilevel exchanges of information, it is valuable to learn how to be flexible in relationships. One way of developing this capacity is by learning how to shift perspective.

Sociodramatic play in childhood, psychodrama, role-playing methods for therapy, education, or recreation offer opportunities for many shifts of viewpoint. There are a variety of role-components utilized in such processes. Children's play, for example, includes such elements as: entering the general context of play, dealing with role distribution, entering the scene and enacting the roles, taking time out when needed, commenting on the interaction, etc. Imagine the shift of roles while you overhear the following: "Let's play." "I'll be the baby and . . ." "No, I want to be the baby." "Okay, you be the baby and I'll be the mommy." "Mommy, give me a cookie!" "Wait, let's get some cookies."

Psychodrama may be viewed as a form of play, since it occurs in a realm of activity where the rules of ordinary reality no longer apply. J.L. Moreno called this context "surplus reality." He was naming that dimension of our lives enriched by our imagination, modified by the psychological and dramatic devices such as condensation, amplification, shifts of attention and role, etc.[8] Ordinary reality, in contrast, can't offer the highlighting and dramatic focus. An abundance of mundane detail can often obscure the significance of an event. Using techniques that create surplus reality, the essential actions can be exaggerated and irrelevant ones eliminated. Furthermore, in the realm of surplus reality, people can interact with their fantasy, memory, and other roles existing only in the mind.

A major benefit of play in therapy, education, and recreation occurs because the basic process of accessing creative solutions, ideas, and actions is learned. Bateson noted how children not only learn about the roles being enacted but, more importantly, they learn that roles can be played, can be manipulated as readily as the putting on and taking off of hats or costumes. Roles may be assumed, modified, refined, elaborated, and relinquished. This is a most liberating lesson. It invites us to reevaluate whatever roles we play, and realize that we are free to create them, renegotiate them with others, or let some parts of them drop away. The ability to do this fosters a capacity for increased responsibility in everyday life.

The Laboratory of Play

Make-believe or sociodramatic play is a natural vehicle of the child's exploration of physical, psychological, and social realities. When children play together, they give each other immediate feedback about each other's enactment. Their comments refer not so much to the artistic refinement of a portrayal so much as its simple accuracy or effectiveness: "Don't go over there, that's where the bad guys hide." "Let's do that again. This time do it this way." The fluid interchange of informal dramatic enactment offers an opportunity to try out a wide variety of approaches, from a coarse rendering of a role to something more subtle. Different styles may be explored. In this sense, play is the child's form of scientific social investigation. Experimentation with various behaviors generates quick feedback regarding their social acceptability, and in this fluid context, they may be relatively easily modified until they achieve some consensual validation.

Play also establishes a context in which otherwise socially unacceptable behaviors are tolerated, if not actually enjoyed. Being silly, crude, seductive, babyish, bossy, mocking of authorities, going beyond the boundaries of propriety—all are common behaviors in the course of sociodramatic enactment. Thus, this realm of surplus reality offers people a relatively fail-safe context for self-expression.

In play, adults can utilize this dimension of drama to explore a wider range of roles. In these enactments, emotions can be expressed and actions experienced that are unavailable in everyday life. For instance, you can take on a wide range of other social and professional roles without all the real requirements. Play allows for an expansion of your role-repertoire far beyond the opportunities afforded in ordinary life.

Expanding Consciousness Through Play

Psychological development, according to the theoretical orientation of role dynamics, is chiefly a process of the mind constantly seeking to expand in new experiences of all kinds—aesthetic, athletic, sensual, creative, expressive, social, intellectual, emotional, imaginative, spiritual, etc. The theory can address this rich and multidimensional quality of the mind better than some of the earlier, more reductionistic psychological systems that focused on themes such as conditioning, discharging tensions, reducing anxiety, or even oversimplified theories of learning. The "co-creative self" is an idea that includes all roles. Moreover, it celebrates the experiences of play and establishes them as equal with the processes of growth in "official" roles.

A related form of consciousness expansion comes with integration. When you discover not only that you can enjoy your eyes and hands, but you can use them together, there is a catharsis of relief and joy as your sense of self expands to include both elements in a synergistic system—"synergy" meaning that the functioning power of the whole is greater than the sum of its parts.[9]

In play, children and adults experience a holistic integration of many components of learning: spontaneous originality, emotional reactions, unconscious motivations, personal temperament and style, social and cultural context, as well as the more researched intellectual processes. Play, therefore, is a primal form of learning by doing, and this complex co-creative process is becoming recognized as one of the most effective forms of education. Participatory, experiential approaches utilizing role-playing are excellent vehicles for learning skills, contexts, expectations, and the roles that embody those elements. Socio-dramatic play is a prime example of an innate type of self-directed education.

The play of childhood extends into many forms as culture adapts these basic needs. Play elements may be found in all areas of human endeavor—scientific research, political campaigns, religious ceremony, business conferences, etc. Yet there should be a place for preserving the basic process of make-believe play as a continuing source of recreation and social involvement. The Art of Play offers a way to do just that.

Nature has a wonderful way of motivating its organisms

through pleasure. In order to ensure the accomplishment of essential tasks, eating is enhanced by taste, and procreation is motivated by sexual tension and enjoyment. The processes of learning and socializing in humans and some of the higher animals are also facilitated by an innate sense of fun that accompanies the freedom to explore alternative actions in the psychosocial context called play. In this special reality there is the opportunity to experience creative possibilities, and for this reason, it should be redeemed as an activity needed beyond childhood and throughout life.

Chapter 3

THE BENEFITS OF PLAY

Imaginative play develops a variety of skills,[1] and your competency in these areas has major psychosocial benefits which may be applied in several aspects of living:

Personal-emotional—enhancing vitality and mental health

Social—strengthening involvements and reducing alienation

Educational—developing the capacity to learn more effectively, and to learn in the broadest sense of the word

Cultural—stimulating the kind of creativity that is required to meet the challenges of a changing world

These dimensions of your living are helped when you augment them with the following component skills:

Flexibility of mind—a broad role repertoire, and a capacity to change set and see various points of view

Initiative and improvisation—a willingness to recognize, modify, and act on your mistakes while cheerfully moving forward

Humility—a sense of humor, an ability to have some objective detachment, a capacity for utilizing criticism

Effectiveness in communication—clear, nonreproachful, constructive, honest, self-disclosing, friendly communication, including the skill of reflective listening

Inclusiveness—an ability to be comfortable in groups, willing to negotiate, support others, mediate, consider everyone's feelings

Questioning—a seeking beyond the obvious, able to "break set" and think of unusual alternatives

Problem-solving—being acquainted with a variety of techniques and strategies

All of these skills are exercised anew in the setting of sociodramatic play. They are constantly utilized in the activities of selecting characters, elaborating scenarios, allowing the implications of each role to be mixed with personal style, and interacting with co-characters in stories so that enjoyable events result. Friction does arise, and learning to work it out in the spirit of cooperation is a major part of the experience.

Personal Benefits

Your personality functions most effectively when it is expanding and/or integrating its roles. Consciousness is nourished by experience, even if it is symbolic, as in fantasy or imaginative play. As J.L. Moreno observed:

> Social life has the tendency to attach a definite role to a specific person, so that this role becomes the prevailing one into which the individual is folded. Everybody is expected to live up to his official role in life—a teacher is to act as a teacher, a pupil as a pupil, and so forth. But

the individual craves to embody far more roles than those he is allowed to act out in life. It is from the active pressure which these multiple units exert upon the manifest official role that a feeling of anxiety is produced. Role playing is then a method of liberating and structuring these unofficial roles.[2]

You get tired, bored or slightly burned out when restricted to living certain dominant roles. Excessive or prolonged enactment of authoritative, submissive, controlling, competent, helping, helpless, or any other general type of role generates a kind of psychic fatigue. It is a relief to engage in an activity that embodies a role that contrasts with a previously extensively enacted role. For example, a teacher may enjoy being a passive student at a continuing-education workshop. On the other hand, a child may enjoy playing the role of a bossy teacher with playmates. Businesses respond to this need by rotating jobs in some factories. It might be a good general principle of group mental hygiene in all businesses for explicit and implicit roles to be clarified and periodically redistributed.

Beyond the healthful aspects of shifting your various roles in real life, there is a deep desire to experience roles you can imagine. You might want to explore being a dragon, a monster, or a bulldozer. Most of us find some identification with the fictional character, Walter Mitty, whose secret life in fantasy is replete with heroic roles. The Art of Play establishes a context within which it is beneficial actually to play those roles in physical enactments with the help of playmates. For instance, if you work at a job that requires you to be a constant and firm disciplinarian, you might want to play roles such as a pampered little baby or shy kitten.

The playful enactment of scenes that offer a shift from overutilized roles and introduce the opportunity for satisfying the desire to expand into a limitless variety of roles results in a kind of healing. The word "heal" is related in its origins in the English language to the word "whole." To balance your roles through actively expressing them generates an experience of wholeness in your psychological existence that nourishes and heals your psyche.

Because many people work and live in contexts where high levels of self-control are the norm, there tends to be a muting of emotions. Prevalent methods of maintaining self-control are found in statements disqualifying feelings: "You shouldn't be reacting this way." "How dare you be angry?" "Stop feeling sorry for yourself." "You should have learned this by now." "Those thoughts are crazy." Commonly repeated inner statements such as these result in a loss of self-esteem and a tendency toward shameful emotional isolation, both of which are tragically unnecessary burdens to add to the realistic stresses in people's lives.

Internal self-suppression is a pervasive situation that results in many movie and television presentations in our culture (and worldwide) that appeal to the need to experience roles expressing great anger, triumph, tragic-but-proud defeat; heroic, and powerful, clear emotions. It is very doubtful that these shows provide any catharsis. Many writers and researchers now propose that the shows actually contribute to the further expression of those emotions.[3] Truly to cleanse the psyche of the accumulated, unclear, inhibited feelings generated in the course of everyday life, people need the opportunity to personally enact their own expressions of events and characters in a socio-dramatic or psychodramatic setting that creates the means and context for catharsis.[4]

Whether the emotions be enacted as they really happened, as in psychodrama, or in a more distanced, symbolic, sublimated form, as in creative dramatic play, there is not only an expression of emotion, but also the additional benefit of validation of the feelings by other people. Furthermore, being in a group with others who are portraying their own chosen scenes provides a vicarious and shared experience. By stimulating each other to play more vigorously and spontaneously, the group process also demonstrates the commonalities of the human condition, and thus counteracts the sense of emotional isolation and "being different."

Social Benefits of Play

A repertoire of noncompetitive, easily performed social activities can be a valuable asset in a busy, impersonal world.

When people engage in spontaneous, imaginative activities, it functions as an enjoyable bonding force. Instead of engaging in subtle social games of one-upmanship, people can discover ways of interacting that reward all the participants. Even in groups of two or three, talking about how you used to enjoy play, and ideas you have about play, can be a pleasurable topic of conversation.

One of the biggest social benefits of imaginative play is that it satisfies both the needs of the group and the needs of the individual. Whereas in many task-oriented groups, the personal idiosyncrasies of the group members are generally ignored or suppressed so there can be a unified effort, in play groups those elements of difference are welcome additions to the process. Since much of the fun comes from seeing how the roles will be elaborated, the originality of each group member adds to the enjoyment of the event. We laugh with shared glee at the unique way George portrays the tiger, and we are delighted with the subtleties Emily shows us in her version of the teddy bear. Thus, make-believe play offers a group format that fosters the expression of the authenticity of each of its participants.

Imaginative enactment provides another benefit by offering a comfortable distancing from the roles of everyday life while still engaging in social interactions. In therapy groups, at parties, or in many meetings, discussion often involves events relevant to the official roles concerning work, love, family and friendships—all "serious" subjects. This gets tiring and boring. It's refreshing to share roles in make-believe play that don't "mean" anything, where no resolution to a problem is required. No one has to be a "helper," "helpee," or authority figure. The playmate role is pleasantly different, and it may be co-created freely to establish the social relationship.

Educational and Cultural Benefits

Perhaps the most valuable aspect of imaginative play is that it fosters creativity. The various component skills are in the same general realm as those noted by a variety of authors who have done research on the phenomenon of creativity. (See Further References on Creativity at the end of this book.) Since around the 1950s a major interest has developed in this subject, no doubt because people had the foresight to realize that creativity was the central skill needed for dealing with what was becoming a society full of ongoing changes. Interestingly, the word "creativity" wasn't even in the dictionary in the early 1930s.[5]

Actual methods for promoting creativity have been limited to more intellectual approaches[6] or indirect techniques.[7] The Art of Play is a method that refines the normal process whereby children develop their creativity, and adapts it for use by adults.

Here at the end of the twentieth century, the global society needs the vast resources of human imaginative energy in the same way it needed sources of physical energy in order to enter the industrial age. Around 200 years ago, that meant a technology had to be developed that could economically tap into, transform, and apply the energy of coal and petroleum. Without such technologies, these materials had been considered relatively worthless. The technology needed and available today can lead us beyond previous tendencies to foster standardized thinking by utilizing our creative resources to develop new solutions and directions. It is becoming generally recognized in many areas of society that there is great value in open-mindedness, intuition, independence of thought, and similar qualities. Fostering such abilities is possible through a synthesis of developments since mid-century or so in group dynamics, sociodrama, psychology, management, education, and other fields.

The qualities that are needed in the coming years are the qualities of **youthfulness**. Ashley Montagu, a noted anthropologist and commentator on contemporary society has discussed this idea at length in his book, *Growing Young*.[8] He points out that the human species exhibits the sociobiological traits of "neoteny" or "paedomorphism." This means humans are designed to optimize the youthful characteristics of the species because these qualities have evolutionary advantages. He has one specific suggestion for implementing his conclusions:

> Hence, the implications of all this should be fully understood and recognized: the importance of the sociodramatic experiences in the life of the child continue into the life of the adult. (p.163)

While Montagu notes how this can be cultivated through promoting some basic behavioral themes, the Art of Play offers a specific method for adults to use in accessing these experiences.

Here, then, is a brief review of the beneficial elements associated with imaginative enactment:

Vehicle for self-discovery

Channel for enhancing vitality and satisfying the desire to enact ideas, events, and characters

Opportunity for shifting, expanding, and balancing roles

Enjoyable recreation and noncompetitive social activity

Mode for broadening role repertoire and developing the skills of empathy

Naturally develops the component skills that foster creativity and experiential learning

Method and context that can satisfy the adult's need for sociodramatic experiences

Chapter 4

AN ORIENTATION TO THE ART OF PLAY

The Art of Play is a new form of recreation—an activity devoted to bringing forth the imaginativeness and spontaneity of its participants. It may also be considered an art form, as discussed in the Introduction. This method is meant to be a friendly, mutually interactive, social experience. We have designed an approach that reduces performance anxiety, because the action occurs only for the benefit of the group of people playing together. Moreover, no effort is made to perfect or even improve the quality of the performance, as would happen in an acting class. The Art of Play is not a specific form of psychotherapy, although there can be therapeutic benefits in a general sense, just as there are in almost any challenging activity. Psychological analysis of the events or the roles portrayed is not useful and is counterproductive to a spirit of relaxed playfulness.

While dramatic enactment or role-playing tends to be the main type of activity we use, it should be noted that other components also are important. Singing or drawing together, experimenting with hats, costumes, or puppets, dancing or moving, and similar forms of structured or spontaneous expressive elements add valuable opportunities for exploration and fun. Indeed, some directors and participants may choose to emphasize the nondramatic activities. The development of enactments or mini-scenarios is a rich but not essential component of the Art of Play. The space devoted to it in this book reflects our own shared arena of expertise and greater interest. Less elaborate enactments or modifications utilizing dance, music, and other forms as a focus can be equally exciting and successful.

Number of Participants

As with other activities, the Art of Play allows for varying degrees of formality, structure, and numbers of people. In its simplest form, you engage in role-taking activities with a friend or family member. This is done by imagining you are in a fantasy role. The other person asks you questions about what it feels like, and then you return the favor by letting your companion come up with an imaginary character. It's fun and simple to be the channel for your personal muse and then to be able to bring forth the spontaneity of the other person. You can do it anywhere and expand it to include three or four people.

Another simple and unstructured use of the Art of Play is to agree in your family to allow people to informally slip into various funny roles around the house. You might bring out a hand puppet and have it interact as if it had come to life. Singing songs in the car when you go for a ride offers a chance to explore singing in different styles. Announcing to your family that you are going to exaggerate your moods by caricaturing them in a role helps you experience new dimensions of something familiar. When friends come over, you may want to invite them to join in some of the activities described in the following pages.

Beyond the home, you can adapt the Art of Play for recreational uses in schools, camps, hospitals, day-care centers, and a variety of other group contexts. In general, it's best to have people play the more complex activities in groups of about six to nine. Larger groups can be introduced to the method through singing together and other component activities; however, for individual enactments, everyone needs to have a chance to participate, and this happens best in smaller groups, of three to five.

Basic Considerations Before You Begin

A fundamental principle in the Art of Play is that group members are not pressured to participate. Play is essentially a voluntary activity. The capacity meaningfully to say yes to participation is predicated on the real freedom to say no. Thus, we allow people to warm up at their own pace, be involved or not in the various activities, and certainly let them leave if they wish.

The length of time a session takes varies with the complexity of the activity. Simple exercises can be enjoyed within the scope of a class period of 50 minutes. More complete enactments require 2 to 3 hours for a comfortable warm-up period, action phase, and closing. We schedule activities in all time frames to optimize participants' exploring and experiencing activities without feeling hurried. The quality of the experience is the focus of a session, rather than staging lots of events.

Levels of experience or abilities of the participants are considered when planning a session. In many ways the Art of Play is similar to other endeavors having "advanced players" and "beginners." Generally, we do not group them together, because the more experience members feel held back and the others feel intimidated.

The Art of Play is as vulnerable to disruptions to group process as other activities; therefore, a level of courtesy, cooperativeness, good humor, and a willingness to speak up are required. Minor and inevitable adjustments of pacing, temperament, and understanding are worked out with tactfully given corrections, encouragement, and gracious receptivity. Occasionally, there will occur moments of friction in which it will be necessary to discuss and openly resolve them. Actually, the methods involved, which include ongoing comments on the process and the necessity for shifting or reversing roles, can be applied to resolve many conflicts. There are times, however, when grossly immature or destructive behaviors require the group to ask a player to leave. This is more likely to happen in contexts where the method is used with disturbed patients.

In small group settings, it's important to help everyone remain somewhat involved. Group members should be encouraged to be open about when they are bored or want to change an activity. Children are very clear on this point, and adults in this kind of activity should not allow false courtesy to create low grade resentment. Indeed, emotional reactions should be shared, because, in truth, we're all more transparent than we might think, and our discomfort is obvious to the sensitive eye or intuitive personality.

The Role of the Director

Spontaneity occurs best within a context of moderate structure. With too little structure, participants experience the ambiguity of the situation as a subtle condition of "overchoice." This results in behaviors ranging from self-consciousness due to vulnerability about misreading what's expected to exuberant activities lacking sensitivity to the consent of the group. Too much structure, of course, restricts opportunities for the expression of creative imagination or original ideas in a playful, experimental way.

Thus, the Art of Play is an activity that requires enough structure to help the group not worry about what's going to be happening, and to focus all participants on relaxing into a playful attitude. A director or group leader must take responsibility for planning and pacing the events of the session, to create an atmosphere that serves the two goals mentioned above. In advanced groups, it's possible the role of director might rotate among the members who would volunteer (with the consent of the others) to lead the next session.

It's important to note that a director does not engage as a participant in the enactments. The group needs the director to sustain a sense of grounding and safety within which the play can happen. In this way, the director's role serves as a symbolic "observing self" for the group, providing a stabilizing and consistent reminder that the roles being enacted are playful and not real. In the theater, this is the healthy buffer zone between reality and fantasy expressed in the statement that no matter how absorbed actors become in the characterizations, they must never completely forget they are acting. The director of the Art of Play helps create that buffer zone by being an involved observer. Therefore, other than the warm-up activities, during which the director can helpfully model a friendly, inclusive level of spontaneity and risk-taking, their exploratory play time should be exercised in other contexts, as participants in someone else's groups, not during their own sessions. An excessively exuberant director will create a passive audience, intimidate, or alienate a group. A mature, caring, and amiable person who likes creating and orchestrating fun activities for others can serve successfully as a director in most settings.

As mentioned earlier, for advanced, sustained enactments (2 to 3 hours) which may very well touch on issues that relate to a participant's personal life, a director trained in some form of group therapy is required. Of course, any groups with obvious mental health concerns must be properly cared for in the same way. Occasionally, even in simple, short sessions, a topic or experience will touch a participant more deeply than expected. It is generally useful to mention this possibility at the beginning of a session, and suggest that if it happens, the individuals make sure they talk about it further with a friend, family member, or even their therapist/counselor if need be. Opportunities for healing and growth present themselves in the context of play and can be welcomed when people are reminded to share their experiences.

Codirectors can be used, each leading separate parts of the session and working together throughout. This is the way we often present the Art of Play. It is much more difficult to establish a comfortable, easy atmosphere when two people direct a session. Similar types of issues that come up in cotherapy also apply to codirectors in the Art of Play. It's important to be actively working on those issues in order to create a successful group experience. Under most circumstances, it is better to have only one director who takes full charge of the group ambience and activities.

The director of adult exploratory play sessions must be competent enough to guide the group through activities that may at times be difficult technically for some individuals. At those times, the director takes on the role of a good teacher and needs to be able to give special attention to help participants find their own levels of comfortable involvement. The director's goal is to maintain an abiding, nonjudgmental presence with an easy, yet attentive concentration on the group, even during free play periods. Staying sensitive to the shifts in spontaneity in the group as a whole gives cues regarding how to pace the activities, possibly changing them to better facilitate the immediate interests of the group, offering additional explanations of how to do an activity, helping subgroups access alternative strategies if they get stuck, etc. In addition, the director designs the experience through activities planned beforehand, and then revises the plan once involvement in the actual event begins. In this way, the director who enjoys creating sessions and reworking the design in a real group context will have the most fun.

Beginning the Session

In the following section, we'll describe some examples of ways we work with our Art of Play groups. Each session is unique, and yet we as group leaders make plans about the kinds of structured experiences we will use. Being aware of the time constraints, numbers of participants, their backgrounds, and their previous experience with this or a related method, we vary the choice of warm-ups and their timing and pacing accordingly.

We share the same priority of maintaining a warm and casual atmosphere, and this requires that we be on friendly terms with each other, be prepared to support one another in our general goals in the face of unexpected events, and be willing to process our interpersonal confusion, disagreements, or need for clarity openly in the group. Our commitment is to engage in and celebrate the spirit of friendship and comfort.

Before people come into the room, we try to arrange chairs or pillows into a loose circle, estimating the group size as closely as possible. If a few people are there already, we introduce ourselves to them personally, facilitate their introductions with each other, and have them help create the circle. We often begin a session with some singing from songbooks that include simple, relatively familiar, and singable, uplifting songs. If people are arriving gradually, offering songbooks is a nice way to receive them.

When the group has assembled, we introduce ourselves, and say a little about what the session will be like. We address the kinds of details that people might have as concerns, such as the times of ending, when the breaks will occur, general norms for the group, etc. One of our norms, for example, is that smokers are asked to restrict their smoking to the breaks. Participants feel more comfortable when they are oriented to the overall activity and have a chance to clarify any pressing questions in the beginning. We tell the group there will be time after the experiential activities for discussions of theoretical and other issues. We've found some people prefer to conclude the session without the intellectual interchange; therefore, we officially end the group early and allow people to leave or stay as they wish.

The experiential warm-up may begin with singing, followed by some movement activities. These can lead into exercises to build group cohesion, and then to activities to stimulate people's imaginations. We might have the participants do some improvisational experiences in pairs (or "dyads"), exchanging partners with each event. In this way, a person gets to have a shared experience with several others, and even a newcomer will feel they have several "allies" in the group.

The Characters Within

The phase of dramatic involvement begins by asking the participants to relax, close their eyes if they wish, and "make an open space" in their mind. We suggest a topic such as an animal, and invite them to allow a character to enter the space. In this first experience we might remind people that a character may become vivid all at once or gradually, starting with a color, a sound, a physical feeling or sensation of movement. This broad approach allows people to find whatever mode of perception best triggers their imagery.[1] We ask them to raise and lower their hand when their character has come to mind, and when most of the group is ready, we have them open their eyes.

Before beginning to go around the circle and asking about the characters, we remind those who may not have a character clearly in mind that it may come during this phase. If it does not, they may simply say, "I pass." We suggest the phrase, "I pass" may be used whenever a participant wishes during the activities throughout the session. We ask the participants to present their character in the following form, "I am . . ." rather than saying, "I thought of . . ." or "I was . . ." This sets the mood for warming up to character enactment. Beginners may respond rather simply, and the first time around we acknowledge each response. It's important for the director to try to be balanced emotionally to each character. This creates a sense of greater inclusion for all kinds of personal images rather than participants subtly creating categories to please the director's tastes. During this phase, responses will be something like, "I'm an eagle," "I'm a unicorn in a field," "I'm a bubbling brook."

We may want to help the group become more fluid in allowing characters to come into their imaginations. In this case, we'll suggest that there are lots of characters to be discovered, we'll repeat the previous exercise using a different theme, and we'll go around again. However, if our time is limited, we may move directly to elaborating details. In order to do this, we ask them to go back into their imaginations with their character in mind and begin to look around at the setting, time of day, what they're made of/have on, and who or what is with/near them. When most people are ready, we have them take turns and share with a partner the details they've discovered. If we have more time, we may go around and have each person present a fuller picture of their character to the whole group.

Here are some responses we have encountered from a variety of categories:

"I'm Mary, Queen of Scots. I have on gorgeous clothes. I'm seventeen, and I'm enjoying flirting with some boys and using my position at court."

"I'm a unicorn with a silver horn. I'm fierce, and I snort like a wild stallion. Only a virgin can tame me."

"I'm a P-40 fighter plane in the 1940s, doing flip rolls at an altitude of 20,000 feet."

"I pass." (Remember, it's all right if someone is not ready. We just move on to the next person with a nod of acknowledgment and a smile.)

"I'm a rock by the side of a brook in a mountain valley. Everything is very peaceful. I can hear someone coming far away."

"My character is . . ." (The director interrupts, reminding the person to speak from the character's voice using "I am . . .") "Okay, I am an eagle, soaring high above a valley . . ."(glancing at two other group members who spoke earlier) . . . "that mountain valley with the brook and the rock." (All three smile.)

"I'm an old accordion, brought over from Europe with an immigrant family. I'm usually wrapped in an old cloth and kept in the closet. I like it best when they bring me out and they play me."

"I'm a garbage collector in Cincinnati."

"I sell apples by the side of a country road. They are magic apples."

After everyone has spoken, we'll go back to the person/s who "passed" and ask if a character has come to mind. Usually the response will be, "Yes, I'm a . . ." If not, we reassure the person/s and the group that in this context "I pass" is a fine answer because the freedom to say yes is based on the freedom to say no. Depending on the experience of the group members, and the time frame, we may then move into enactments of one character at a time.

If we're with beginners, we ask one or two questions in order to draw out more specifics about the character, which also models the kinds of questions that are helpful to ask. For example, we might ask the person who was an apple vendor how old she is, what sex, or what clothes she is wearing. (We don't assume that people have to take roles that are the same sex as they are in real life—it's part of the process of role-expansion to allow characters of the opposite sex to come to mind and genderless ones like "a mountain," "the north wind," etc.) We would ask the rock or the airplane appropriate questions such as, "What color rock are you?" and "What's the weather like at 20,000 feet?" We certainly do not ask "Why did you pick that character?" "Why" questions are a sure way of killing spontaneous play in a group because everyone will withdraw in fear of judgment and uninvited analysis of their thoughts and behaviors. The director must refocus the group whenever a "why" comes up by saying something like, "We're not interested in 'why's' in this group. Now let's get back to the character."

In order to develop the skill of role creativity, we often have the group do an exercise in which they break into pairs, and one person in each pair elaborates their character while the other person asks questions aimed at helping the character to become more vivid. After about 5 to 10 minutes, we tell them to switch roles, and the person who came up with the first character now asks the questions of the partner's character.

Taking a Break

In longer sessions, we pause after about an hour to allow people to have time for their own needs. The aim is to take a break before the participants become overly uncomfortable. During this time, people can leave the room to go to the bathroom, smoke a cigarette (we have no smoking in the playroom), explore the area, get a drink of water, make phone calls, ask questions, interact informally with other group members, etc. Often, a few group members use this opportunity as an occasion to initiate some spontaneous form of play together. We facilitate this relaxation of focus, because it imparts a less goal-directed and more casual feeling in the room.

After the break, we often change modalities, which is a refreshing way to show there are many ways to play. Perhaps we'll do the "draw a mandala" activity mentioned in Chapter 9. Group members help in passing around the crayons and papers. We might introduce the method by calling it doodling. As they take turns, there's usually giggling and a variety of comments. After about 10 minutes, we ask them to wind it up in 2 minutes or so. When the dyads are finished, we encourage people to walk around and see what the other pairs of players did. We keep the drawings available but off to the side. At the end of the session, we offer to keep the drawings, or people may take them home.

The Enactment Phase

In extended sessions of 2½ to 3 hours, and with more advanced groups, we move steadily into individual enactments. This approach is discussed and examples are presented in the next chapter. For beginners, large groups, and in limited time frames, we allow smaller subgroups to play together for experimentation and practice. We may have the subgroups choose one person's character to enact for the larger group. In this case, everyone else in the subgroup releases their own character in order to play co-characters in the chosen person's enactment. Each group decides what they will enact, what characters there will be, etc. This process allows the main character to be elaborated. Another technique offering enactment possibilities for everyone is to have each person imagine being a character in a common setting, such as a forest. People are asked to place themselves in the room as if it's the forest; the director has them share with the group who or what they are; and then they are allowed to find ways to play together based on who/what is in the forest.

Ending a Session

After enactments and group participatory exploration of characters, we begin to end the session by bringing the group together as a whole. This may be done by offering some more

singing or other simple, easy activities. Often the final enactment can create a closing, such as watching each subgroup
present their imaginary characters in scenes.

We remind people to share with a friend or others any
material that seems to deserve more attention. As a way of
saying thank you, we acknowledge the gifts the group members have given each of us by sharing their characters, which
are like poems. We encourage the participants to take this
type of playfulness back to their families, friends, and col-
leagues. Finally, we conclude by reminding people that time
has been allotted here at the end for those who would like to
stay and talk with us about the session or ideas they had. The
group disbands and informally completes unfinished good-
byes and intellectual needs.

Themes of Play

The challenge of sociodramatic play comes by taking on
a role that is to some extent unfamiliar. Portraying a person
of the opposite sex, a different age, or even from another culture can be an invigorating exercise for your imagination. It's
fascinating to enact what it might be like to be an animal,
plant, or even an inanimate object.

The Art of Play benefits from the cultivation of a variety
of approaches, the first of which will be described in the following pages, and the others in Chapters 6 through 9. The
factors below overlap and interweave at all ability levels;
however, it is obvious that some of these areas will become
especially interesting at the intermediate and advanced levels.

Exploring needs and themes of imaginative play
Cultivating receptivity to your imagination
Improvising scenes
Learning techniques to enrich role creativity
Ways of expanding dramatic experience
Integrating other expressive modalities

A Closer Look at Enactments

The two basic goals of imaginative play involve the satisfaction of: the desire to enact ideas, events, and characters (real and imaginary) as described in Chapter 3, and the motivation to discover the dynamic potentials inherent in the development of roles. In the first case, the person who becomes the main character has the experience of portraying their area of interest in order to fulfill their desires. In the second case, the player takes a role to experience it as a pure act of curiosity and creativity. Here are some specific references that will help as we expand on these themes. The following roles were chosen by participants in our sessions of the Art of Play:

A queen, picking her consort

A five-year-old child, having her most perfect birthday

A cruel slave master on a galley ship

An American Indian, preparing for his "vision quest"

A mountain climber, talking with the mountain

A group of spacemen landing on a strange planet

Miss Piggy, entertaining Kermit the Frog as her suitor

A monster, destroying and devouring a city

One of Santa Claus's uncooperative elves

A businesswoman, being wined and dined as a consultant

Styles: Each of the main characters—the group members who played the central roles—choose the style for the scenes. Here are some options for your enactments:

"Straight"—simply elaborating the role in a somewhat true-to-life fashion and seeing what follows.

"Hamming it up"—exaggerating the characterization, the role becomes a vehicle for silly, sexy, nasty, fierce, or other extreme behavior.

"Replay"—repeating the central elements several times, in order to experiment with different styles of play or approaches to the situation.

Seriously—seeking to discover the deeper feelings and issues involved with a role, and to resolve the conflicts inherent in that role.

Heightening the desired effect—replaying an aspect of a scene, such as being even more gloriously triumphant, more lavishly pampered, or more dramatically "dying."

Role reversal—becoming one of the other roles in the scene in order to investigate the experience of being someone or something else.

Part of the pleasure of this kind of play arises out of the surprising richness that emerges—the humor, pathos, complexity, power, grace, and tenderness that accompanies the spontaneous elaboration of a character in action. You'll find it's easy to discover the wealth of imagery and creativity available after the short journey into your imagination.

Co-characters: In addition to being the main character who functions as a kind of codirector and playwright, it is very rewarding to take the roles of the co-characters in other people's enactments. Thus, if someone wanted to be the main character in the scene of Miss Piggy, you might volunteer to play the co-character of Kermit the Frog or one of her servants.

Not only does each character have aesthetic and intellectual dimensions that are interesting, but each role-relationship has its implicit co-characters with unique qualities. For example, the person playing the American Indian asked for several co-characters, such as a wise medicine man and a very old man in the tribe. Wonderful subtleties can arise as the relationships unfold naturally, based on the elements in a scene and the spontaneity of the other players. The improvisation of the participants can be as engrossing to witness as a jam session of accomplished jazz musicians.

The audience: In the process of imaginative play, you can also help co-create scenes as a member of the audience during someone else's enactment. The role of the audience in small group activities is significant in itself. Remember the nice feeling of being able to put on little skits for people when you were a child. The audience is a fundamental part of all traditional cultural celebrations. Furthermore, you might become part of a Greek chorus, a rooting section, a source of catcalls and boos, as in some of those old-fashioned melodramas, or be asked to join a scene as a participant after it evolves in new directions.

As we've said before, this method can be fun, similar to the kind that actors experience, or people who engage in sports. Allow the sense of fun to be your guide, and yet play seriously, as children do when they're really involved in their make-believe enactments. When it stops being fun for you, take responsibility to renegotiate your involvement. Remember to start with simpler role-taking activities, on relatively uncomplicated issues, and move gradually toward an intermediate level. Develop your own psychological and social skills in other areas if you want to go on to more advanced Art of Play exercises. Use the role-playing experiences to build your capacity to empathize with a broad range of roles. The skills you develop will help you in your everyday life, whether as friend, spouse, parent, teacher, manager, psychotherapist, actor, coworker, planetary citizen, or in many other "official" roles. The truth about who you are is that you contain vast resources for role-playing. Your imaginative dimensions are as real a part of your essence as your ordinary interactions in everyday life.

The next chapter will describe in more detail an example of the kinds of extended enactments that have occurred in the Art of Play. Remember, however, that your play sessions may be similar to the examples mentioned in this chapter. Simple and less formal groups following the basic principles of creating a safe and comfortable environment for adult exploratory play offer a valuable addition to social experiences in many contexts.

Chapter 5

THE EXTENDED SESSION—
AN EXAMPLE

For experienced participants in a group of eight to ten people, and when there are at least 2½ to 3 hours of time, the enactment of one character at a time becomes possible. We begin the session with a warm-up phase and move directly into imagining characters. It's fine if there are two or more characters with the same identity, such as Joan of Arc, because each player will bring to the portrayal certain themes and a style that expresses their own individuality. For example, we have discovered that the age and events of several Joans of Arc in a group will tend to be different and offer great variety. During these recreational play experiences, we never worry about the historical accuracy of an enactment that involves historical figures. The spontaneity of the participants will be significantly inhibited if accuracy is expected. Furthermore, the group can become caught up in arguments over facts. The emphasis in our sessions is on developing the imagination, and the historical character merely offers cues with which the participant can stimulate further play. (However, one could adapt the role-playing idea to teaching history, in which case accuracy would be expected—but that will be discussed further in Chapter 13.)

Due to time constraints, everyone who wants to explore an enactment might not be able to do so at a particular session. It's important to remember some of the enactments can be quite satisfactory though lasting only a few minutes. The director should allow only what needs to be played, with no sense of having to create a complete theatrical scene or play. Enactments can involve a number of other players as co-characters and last a half hour or more. In an ongoing group, over a series of sessions, the opportunities to enact a character get distributed evenly. The chances to be someone else's co-character offer everyone a turn to play in each session.

If there are more than 10 people, we consider breaking the group down into subgroups of four to six and encouraging them to work out some mini-enactments themselves. The process of people planning an improvisational skit is also enjoyable.

The group chooses which of the characters will be explored in an enactment. This process involves how much any particular group member/s wants to enact their character, as well as how interesting it is to the group. If several participants want to go first, it is easy to simply vote on it. Sometimes enactments require only a few minutes, at other times a leisurely buildup of the action helps facilitate the main character's exploration.

The person who presents their imaginary scene is called the main character, even if they explore other roles during their enactment. In general, we try to keep each enactment to a maximum length of 30 minutes. Following the selection of a participant as the main character, we have them briefly describe who they are and who/what else is important in the scene. We then move immediately into catalyzing the main character's action and interaction with their co-character/s. Narrating what's happening is immediately redirected by our suggesting, "Show us," and "Do it, rather than telling us about it."

Setting Up a Scene

In this first example, the director facilitates the scene for two intermediate players, Allen and Betty. (All names are fictional and are assigned in alphabetical order.) Allen as the main character, the one who chose the scene, will be called Player 1, or "P1." Betty is the co-character, and will be called Player 2, or "P2." Note how the players are helped to warm up gradually. At one point, the director uses the technique of role reversal to help P2 learn how to play the role the way P1 envisions it. Allen joins the director in front of the group and it proceeds like this:

Director: "Who are you?"
Player l: "I'm Sir Lancelot and I'm talking to Queen Guine-
vere."
D: "Where are the two of you?"
P1:   "I think we're in her study, or something like a study."
D: "In the castle?"
P1:   "Yes, and she has on fine, regal clothes."
D: "Okay, pick someone to be Guinevere."
P1:   (Allen looks around and asks Betty) "Will you?"
P2:   "Sure." (Betty gets up and enters scene.)
D: "Let's set up the study. Where is Guinevere?"
P1:   "She's on a couch—sort of half reclining . . . over here."
D: "Let's take two or three chairs and make something to
sit on with her feet up." (Several people help get chairs and
set it up.)
P2:   (out of role) "This is going to be easy—I get to relax!"
P1:   (continuing the joking) "Oh yes, you lie around a **lot!**
You're the **Queen!**"
D: "Where are you, Lancelot?"
P1:   Well, I've just entered the room."
D: "From where?"
P1:   "Over there—it's sort of like a portal with heavy
drapes."
D: "Does Guinevere know you're coming?"
P2:   "Sure I do—he comes every day at this time!" (Group
laughs.)
P1:   "Yeah, but I'm here to discuss something important
about the King—Arthur, you know."
D: "Okay, Guinevere, did you hear that? He's here to dis-
cuss some important business with you today."
P2:   "Yes, but what business?"

D: "We'll let Lancelot tell you, and let the scene begin with his entering over there through the heavily draped portal."

P1: "Hello, Guinevere. I'm sorry I'm so late but I had to check something out before I came."

P2: (sexy voice) "You're never too late, Lancelot. I *love* it whenever you get here." (Group laughs.)

P1: (a bit confused by the seductive approach, laughs with group, but can't seem to find the way back to his original idea)

D: "Lancelot, is that the way you'd like Guinevere to respond?"

P1: "Well, not exactly."

D: "Guinevere, in order to help you get into Lancelot's idea of how to play this role, let's role-reverse for a minute and Allen (Pl) will lie here on the couch and show you the way he'd like her to respond to Lancelot. You just watch." (P2 agrees.)

P1: (on couch, reclining) "I'm Guinevere now?" (D nods.) (jumps up when imaginary Lancelot enters room and speaks in a worried voice) "Oh, Lancelot, I thought something was wrong! You're *never* late!"

D: "What does Lancelot say then?"

P1: "He tells her about a plot he's discovered to kill King Arthur."

D: "And Guinevere's response is . . ."

P1: "She says . . ."

D: (interrupting) "Say it from Guinevere's role, in her own words."

P1: "Okay . . . uh . . . (as Guinevere) Are you sure? Who is it?"

D: "That's fine. Thank you. (to P2) Guinevere, would you like to begin again with Lancelot entering the room, you jump up from the couch, say you were worried, and then let Lancelot tell you about the plot?"

P2: "Okay, I've got it now." (gets on the couch)

P1: (going to the portal) "Guinevere, I'm sorry I'm late!"

P2: (jumps up and runs to Lancelot) "Oh, my darling, I was so worried about you!"

P1: "I've discovered some dreadful news!"

P2: "What?"
P1: "There's a plot to kill King Arthur!"

The play continues without much further help from the director. Lancelot and Guinevere share some poignant moments about their loyalties and love for King Arthur, and their conflicting dream of freedom to continue their love affair. The scene ends when Lancelot and Guinevere embrace in sadness and fear. Allen looks up and says, "That's it."

Notice how the movement between adjustments in the roles is fluid, emphasizing the creative process rather than a finished performance. More advanced players might move into roles more fully, with fewer directions; however, it's important to know how to help someone warm up gradually in order to allow the emergence of their imagination.

Experienced players sometimes codirect their own scenes if they want to modify the co-character's behavior. Player 1 might have said, "Wait—I'd rather you played it another way. Let's role-reverse and I'll show you . . ."

Trying Something New

Here's an example that illustrates how the Art of Play also can function as a vehicle for experiencing something totally new. The main character is Catherine, again designated P1:

D: "And who are you?"
P1: "I'm a famous jazz singer performing at the Hollywood Bowl. It's a one-night special—very big."
D: "Where are you when your scene opens?"
P1: "I'm onstage, singing, really transported, you know . . . it's a great moment . . . the audience is really with me."
D: "Is there someone in particular in this scene with you? In the band, or audience, or backstage?"
P1: (thinking) "No. Just me and the audience."
D: "Would you like the group to play the audience?"
P1: "Yes . . . but I have to tell you something: I can't sing!"
D: "You, the jazz singer, or you in real life?"

P1: "In real life."

D: "That doesn't have to matter in this imaginary scene. Would you like to play the jazz singer as you described it?"

P1: "Sure, but I can't sing!"

D: "There are techniques we can use to help with that. Since this is for your benefit, and we're imagining it, we can have everyone sing with you, and you can sing, but you won't have to sing all alone. How would that be?"

P1: "That would help—sure."

D: "Okay, let's go back to the stage . . . what do you have on?"

P1: "Mmm, it's slinky, really gorgeous . . . I've got a great figure . . . and I'm not too old . . ."

D: "How old are you?"

P1: "Well, I've been singing for—well, professionally for . . . since I was fifteen, and I'm forty-two now, so everybody knows me by now . . ."

D: "Okay. What's the weather like?"

P1: "It's night outside, of course, and summer; hot, but not too hot—just right, warm and relaxed—the weather. I mean, not me!" (laughs)

D: "What do you as the forty-two-year-old jazz singer do to relax before you go onstage for a big concert? What works after all these years?"

P1: "I pray!" (laughs nervously)

D: "Let's begin the scene before the concert, when you are alone somewhere and take a moment by yourself to pray."

P1: "Okay, it might help."

D: "Where might you be?"

P1: "I'm in my dressing room with the door locked."

D: "Please set up a bit of the dressing room in this area."

P1: "Yeah, well . . . I'm at my mirror, all made up. I'm beautiful. I'm sitting in front of it and looking at myself." (Catherine pulls up a chair and sits with her back to the audience.)

D: "Let's have the mirror face this way with your side to the group, so they see you in profile, okay?"

P1: "Yes. I don't need a table, that's too much trouble."

D: "Are your arms at your sides, or . . . ?"

P1:   "Well, they're really on the table, my elbows."

D: (to another group member) "Will you bring the table over, please?" (to Player 1) "How are you feeling tonight, other than nervous?"

P1:   (Table arrives during this imagining.) "Oh, I'm well and feeling good. I always prepare myself before a big concert. I eat right for the week before, get enough sleep, like I'm in training." (table in place)

D: "Okay, here's your dressing table. Let's begin with your looking in the mirror, and would you speak out loud about what you see and what you are thinking?"

P1:   "I have a kind of glow about me. I really love singing and I love people—the audience. I have a talent for reaching them, personally, even when I'm far away, up on the stage. I'm beautiful, but it's also deep down—I've always had that beauty since I was little . . ."

D: "Are you still nervous about the performance?"

P1:   "Oh, yes, and that's why I pray." (Warmed up, she bows her head into her hands, elbows on table; she needs no further prompting.) "Dear Lord. Well, here I am, another night, to sing for these wonderful people. You have been by my side so many nights and days, and I know you'll be there tonight when I need you. I'm scared, Lord; it's such a big responsibility to get out there and give them my best. You always come to ease that fear. I know I'm singin' for you and you're singin' with me. Thank you for your presence in my life, and especially again tonight. Amen." (slowly raises her head and looks up at the director)

D: "Would you like to sing now with the group singing along with you?" (She nods in assent; director takes the player's hand and she rises.) "Let's move the table and chair away." (Player 1 does that and comes back.) "Before any singer sings, they often warm up; so let's all warm up together by singing a simple chorus or two." (To Player 1) "Do you have one you like?"

P1:   "Uh, yeah, *Let the Sunshine In* . . . from *Hair*."

D: "Okay, you begin and we'll join in."

P1:   (clears her throat) "Let's see, uh, 'Let the sunshine . . .'" (Director and several others pick up the cue and join in.)

All: "Let the sunshine in, the sunshine in . . ." (They continue for about a minute and stop.)

D: "Do you want to warm up with another?"

P1: "No, I'm ready to go out there."

D: "All right. Show us where you are and go ahead."

P1: "It's just a big, empty stage. The orchestra's down there in the orchestra pit, and all the lights are on me and I'm singing."

D: "What are you singing?"

P1: "Well, it's not really a jazz song, but what came to my mind is *People*, the one Barbra Streisand did."

D: "Please say the words you'll sing, so we can remember them."

P1: "I'll try." (coughs) "People, people who need people, are the luckiest people in the world. One person . . ." (forgets words)

Group Member: (calls out) "One very special person . . ."

P1: (flashes a smile, getting into it) "Yeah, 'A feeling deep in your soul, says you were half, now you're whole'. . ." (to end of chorus)

D: "Great!" (to group) "Do we have it, to sing along?"

Group: "Yes!"

D: "Okay. Do you walk out on the stage or are you already there?"

P1: "I'd like to walk out and have everyone clap and cheer."

D: "Okay, it's all yours." (Player 1 backs off to enter; director plays role of announcer) "And now, ladies and gentlemen, here she is!!" (Group cheers and claps enthusiastically.)

P1: (slowly walks forward) "It's great to be here tonight. I want to start with . . ." (breaks out of character and turns to director) "I can't do this—everyone's looking at me!"

D: "Well, there's another technique we can use if it will help you. The group will sing along so that you don't sing alone, and you can face away from them and close your eyes, and imagine you are there on the stage of the Hollywood Bowl."

P1: (turns around and faces the wall) "Yes, I can do it then. Okay, where was I?" (back in character) "I want to start with a song about who you all are to me." (clears throat)

D: (gives a hand cue to the group to get ready to sing along
     with Player 1)
P1: (begins to sing tentatively and the group joins in) "Peo-
     ple, people who need people . . ." (to end of song)

At the end, Catherine is shaking and smiling. She shares
with the group that it is the first time she has ever sung aloud
outside of her shower. The group also shares their own feelings of appreciation for her scene and their own stagefright.

Facilitating the Action

Another example shows how the director helps to move
along a scene involving an advanced player. It gets stuck in
prolific yet repetitive dialogue. Don (P1) volunteers to explore his character:

D: "Who are you?"
P1: "I am the Duke of Padua on the way to meet the father
     of the prospective groom for my daughter. I have a sword
     and a cape." (brandishes an imaginary sword and swirls an
     imaginary cape) "It's a clear crisp day in the autumn, and
     I'm passing friends going to the tavern . . ." (waves at
     imaginary friends)
D: "Would you pick someone to be the father of the pro-
     spective groom?"
P1: "I want someone to volunteer."
D: "Okay, who wants to . . ."
P2: "Me!" (Elizabeth interrupts the director and jumps up.)
D: "Duke, this is the father of the prospective husband for
     your daughter. All right?"
P1: "Sure, but she's prettier than my daughter! (laughs,
     breaking out of character somewhat)
D: (to group) "In imaginary enactments, as we've said be-
     fore, people don't have to play their own sex or age—we
     can be anything. So, Duke, who is this gentlemen?"
P2: "I'm the Count of Cost-a-lotsi!"
P1: (amused) "Sure!"
D: "How do you want the Count to be played?"

P1: "Anyway she wants."

P2: "My dear Duke! I hear your ships had a successful journey to the New World!"

P1: "Yes, thank you. I've paid off all my debts and I'm ready to celebrate . . . with a wedding, perhaps?"

P2: "Indeed? Perhaps so. Let us first celebrate, as you say, with some ale at the tavern."

P1: "Yes, Count, we do have matters of some importance to discuss together."

They get chairs and a table, and sit down. They ad-lib getting ale from a waitress, clink glasses, and start to drink. A variety of exchanges unfold regarding the dowry and other financial issues that border on repetitive haggling. There seems to be little further character development or dramatic progress.

D: (interrupting players to introduce a catalytic technique) "Okay, let's imagine that you've been talking for an hour, and you've had a few too many glasses of ale. What might happen?"

Player 1 initiates a quarrel, and Player 2 leaves in a huff, saying he won't agree to the marriage. The action is stopped with Player 1 not knowing where to take it.

D: "At this point, Duke, perhaps you might have a conversation with someone else about what just happened in the tavern—your wife or daughter or someone else."

P1: "Yes, I'll talk to my wife."

The action continues, using several other psychodramatic techniques to help the events unfold. For instance, in a later scene, a player volunteers to be the daughter, but can't think of anything to say once she is in the scene. Don role-reverses with her to offer some ideas. At another point, the Duke uses the technique of asides to tell what he is not saying to his daughter. A soliloquy is delivered in which the Duke expresses sadness over losing his daughter and ambivalence regarding her preferring to be with the Count's son rather than stay with the family. The mood of enactment, which began on a comedic level, shifts toward more seriousness and tenderness. Finally, the Duke returns to a scene with the Count, they reconcile and seal the marriage agreement over another round of ale.

Enactments of All Sizes

This last example described a rather long and complex enactment, yet it sustained the interest of a group of intermediate and advanced players. This type of play requires more experience and talent from the director. It also needs several group members who are able to be co-characters. However, even with experienced players, enactments can be very simple. The possibility of short, low-excitement explorations must always be invited and validated. A group can enact several small scenes in less than an hour, and then enter another period of imagining new characters before the session has ended.

After a scene has released its peak energy, there will inevitably be a drop in the impetus of action. The shift of energy or level of excitement in the group can be easily sensed. When this happens, either the director, the main character, or a member of the audience can feel free to stop the scene. In fact, learning to respond to the shifts in spontaneity is an important part of the Art of Play. At those times there should be a corresponding shift in the activities of the group. The director can ask the main character, as primary player, "Do you feel finished?" If the answer is "No," the director and player discuss what experience is needed. The player might say, for example, "I need to have something happen that bolsters my pride." After a moment's thought, the player might suggest a closing event. If they need a suggestion, the director can ask the group members to offer ideas. Sometimes the group conversation itself is enough to complete the player's need for closure.

Through all of these events, the director should maintain a gentle and noncontrolling attitude, trusting the players' sense of when completion has happened. The needs of the group as a whole must also be kept in mind. Therefore, the director tries to keep a balance by monitoring the group's level of engagement in the enactment. And finally a reminder we want to stress again—an enactment does not need to conform to literary or theatrical requirements to constitute a coherent production.

The Value of Replay

The technique of replay can be a useful closing technique. For example, following the last scene involving the Duke of Padua, the director would ask, "Does anyone want to play their version of a part of the enactment?" One of the group members replies, "I wanted to be the daughter and object to the marriage! I didn't choose the groom; my mother did, and she lied to the Duke!" A brief encounter is then staged between the Duke, played by the original player—or by someone else, if they don't want to continue the role—and the new player enacting her version of the Duke's daughter.

The replay phase of the action in a session tends to bring the group energy to a more ordinary level, and thus prepares people for winding down the session as a whole. It can be a useful technique if the director senses a high level of involvement by group members in the audience role. Replay gives others a chance to bring their ideas into action. Replay also can be offered to the main character to allow them to explore several angles of an event.

As part of the closing, we remind group members to talk with one another or a friend in order to come out of their imaginary characters if they feel a need to clear their involvement in a role that has been very involving. As a general rule, however, the various activities in the Art of Play and the action in the scenes of other players naturally tends to dissipate the participants' need to continue enactments.

To close a session, we may sing a few songs in a circle as an acknowledgment of the group experience. Typically, some informal question-and-answer exchanges continue to take place even after the session has formally ended.

An Outline of an Extended Session

A general idea of our approach to a session of sustained enactment is presented below. This process may be modified to appeal to the interests of different groups, such as musicians, dancers, visual artists, etc. Creative arts teachers, therapists, and teachers in other disciplines may choose to emphasize their own areas of expertise. An ongoing group may choose to modify a session by playing freely with creative materials and take a break from sociodramatic enactment or other structured events. Otherwise, the session follows this general order of activities:

1. Warm-up, led by director:
    a. Welcome, introductions, address the basic ground rules.
    b. Brief group activities to increase mental and physical involvement, stimulate the imagination, and build group cohesion and trust.
    c. Director introduces the general method, describes the process, notes the terminology and clarifies what's going to be happening. Encourage openness and the freedom to ask questions. Didactic phase is brief and focused on orientation. Refrain from talking about it at the expense of allowing the group to do it.
2. Evoke Character from the Imagination:
    a. Director leads the group in getting in touch with their imaginary characters. Encourage participants to allow roles to come to mind spontaneously, or with the aid of given themes, hats, props, masks, or other techniques to stimulate the imagination.
    b. Characters may be specific (i.e., *Julius Caesar, Juliet*), or general (i.e., a Roman soldier, a medieval merchant's daughter).
    c. Common categories that help us focus the imagination include:

family   animals, plants   history (or future)
occupations   myth, legend   inanimate objects
movies, TV   stories, comics

    d. Develop characters. Slowly add more dimensions, such as:

age	setting	clothing/appearance
sex	time	likes/dislikes

3. Establish Scene:
   a. Utilize the principles of character elaboration as described in Chapter 7:
      (1) Be subjective: "...I ..."
      (2) Use the present tense: "I am ..."
      (3) Describe a specific situation: "I am here ..."
      (4) Emphasize emotional states: "I am feeling ..."
      (5) Amplify characterization: "I am also feeling ..."
      (6) Express the unspoken: "What I'm not saying aloud is ..."
      (7) Focus on the relationship: "With you I feel ..."
   b. Begin to move physically in the staging area, defining the space: "Here's the sofa, there's the door ..."
   c. Establish background of scene, concerns, hopes, fears.
   d. Invite co-characters into the scene; have them warm up to their role; use role reversal with the main player to clarify their character, if asked.
4. Develop the Enactment:
   a. Explore the dimensions of the relationships between the characters in the scene, such as conflicts, style of play, types of pleasures, and related events.
   b. Use various techniques to explore the scene, such as creative use of movement, physical contact, position, or posture; exaggerations; shifts of character, scene, time or place; and other dramatic vehicles mentioned in Chapter 8.
   c. Experiment with a variety of kinds of outcomes, such as funny, feared, desired, or most expressive.
   d. Integrate other modes of play as listed in Chapter 9.
5. Expand the Enactment (For intermediate or advanced players):
   a. Deepen the characterization and the encounter.

    b. Explore the processes of conflict resolution.

6. Replay and Discussion.
    a. Invite others to play the scene.
    b. Allow clarifications, but not judgmental or psychological analysis.
    c. Warm up for another enactment.
    d. Make a clear closure, either for a break or for ending the group:
      (1) Discuss any unfinished issues; answer questions.
      (2) Exchange goodbyes. Be clear about the time and place of further meetings.

In the next four chapters we'll present further techniques and approaches to building basic role-playing skills and enriching your enactments.

Chapter 6

FUNDAMENTALS OF ENACTMENT

Sociodramatic imaginative enactments benefit from the practice of a few basic skills. In this and the following chapters we'll discuss some principles that you may find helpful. We begin with the cultivation of your imagination so that warming up to spontaneous improvisation will flow more naturally.

The Art of Play involves a way of thinking that is closer to the musings of the poet than the calculations of an engineer. Likewise, therapeutic, educational, or recreational improvisational drama is different from activities that involve more rational planning. These activities that involve creative role-taking require the participant to become receptive to the subtle imagery and cues of intuition bubbling up continuously from the subconscious. It's important to be clear about how the two approaches contrast, because imaginative skills are somewhat different from the dominant modes of thinking validated in our society. Indeed, there are a number of psychosocial resistances to imaginative, spontaneous role-playing (which are analyzed in Chapters 10 through 12).

Thinking versus Imagining

In many fields of study, there has been a growing recognition that during the last few centuries the Western worldview became somewhat distorted, overvaluing certain aspects of existence and devaluing or even ignoring other aspects. Recent advances in neurophysiology have helped clarify this distortion and have led to speaking in terms of people using "both sides of their brains".[1] Although the scientific details don't fit all the generalizations, models of the mind (and of culture) have been proposed that offer a clearer picture of the various functions of the two dimensions. The left side of the brain tends to be described as the source of mathematics, language, and "convergent thinking," while the right sides seems to be more capable in functions such as emotion, intuition, imagination, aesthetics, and "divergent" modes of thought.[2]

Most Western educational experiences have tended to emphasize the cultivation of left-brained abilities, while the realms of imagination have been neglected or distrusted. Learning to think in terms of roles and scenarios cultivates the right-brained qualities. Sometimes this requires unlearning habitual patterns of relying on objective evidence and thinking in overly abstract categories.

Here's an illustration of the two different modes of thought. Remember how in school you might be asked a question something like this: "What are three uses of a gasoline-powered engine?" (As an exercise, try answering this question before reading further.) Your mind probably went through a computerlike search for the definitions of the terms, the retrieval of categories and examples, and checking to see how the answers could be phrased to answer the question adequately. It feels a bit like going to a little library in your head, and focusing your attention on an internalized card catalog. That exercise is a left-brain experience.

In contrast, at storytelling time, the teacher might begin, "In the middle of a deep forest . . ." and immediately a vision was projected onto the mental "screen" in every child's mind. (Again, try this out—what kind of forest do you see in your mind's eye?) Of course, each child probably saw a slightly different forest, depending on their experience and a host of other factors. Perhaps some pictured forests with large trees, spaced apart, with a relatively clear, low-lying ground cover; others may have envisioned a thick underbrush and many closely spaced trees. The time of day, season, evidence of animal life varied from person to person, and the images themselves came without effort.

This flow of spontaneous imagery can be auditory and kinesthetic as well as visual. You can hear and feel things in your imagination, as well as see them. (With a little practice, you can learn to smell and taste in your imagination, also.) The stimuli are there all the time, and all you have to do is to allow your attention to move gently toward any theme. For example, if you listen intuitively, you may discover one or more melodies circulating somewhere around in the back of your mind. If you listen in a receptive state of mind, as if you were listening to a distant sound of a bird or insect, you'll probably detect it. It may be familiar or unfamiliar, associated with the words of a song, or purely melodic. Similarly, in a relaxed state, you can move your attention around without twitching a muscle. For example, right now, direct your attention to your left big toe. You can feel it more vividly. Now shift the attention to your right ear. Moving your awareness around your body or from one subtle sound to another becomes less elusive the more you practice.

The process of focusing attention occurs most readily in a state of relaxation rather than a state of effort. "Trying" is a psychophysiologic process that includes a rise in muscle tension in several major muscle groups. In stress-reduction clinics, the technique of biofeedback is used to help clients become aware of these slight forms of tension. In states of relaxation, clients may also be helped to use their imagery to alter their pulse, blood pressure, and the temperature of their fingertips. Guided imagery is used along with biofeedback, and the point of the exercise is to allow the body naturally to follow the imagination. This is called "passive volition." Instead of actively trying to warm their own hands, clients may be instructed to imagine lying in the warm sun on a pleasant beach, and that sense of internal permission seems to allow the blood vessels to relax and open.[3] The mind is incredibly, constantly alive, a veritable fountain of fantasy, hopes, memories, associations, and all sorts of other ideas. This is the root of spontaneity, inspiration, and humor. It can be tapped as the source of imaginative activity, which is what people do in the professions based on creative expression.

In addition to its prolific generation of material, the subconscious mind is amazingly quick and ingenious at converting essentially meaningless stimuli into meaningful patterns. For example, have you ever noticed how, in the course of dreaming, if a phone bell should ring, your mental processes can convert it into something with a bell ringing as part of the dream? By weaving new stimuli into meaningful contexts, the mind can thus preserve the flow of dreaming. This rapid transformation and redefinition of novel material is what also happens when children play, and no effort is expended. You don't have to "try" to play—when you're warmed up enough, your spontaneity will flow. As you familiarize yourself with the processes of cultivating this dimension, you'll be pleasantly surprised at how effortless it becomes. The more you practice, the easier it gets.

The tendency of the mind to find meaningful patterns in things is very close to its natural ability to create stories. For instance, dream interpretation has a heritage that goes beyond recorded history. Similarly, the theory-building at the frontiers of modern science, reflect the ability of the mind to make sense of what might seem random at first view. The spontaneous flow of imagery and the inclination toward converting those stimuli into stories leads to an innate ability for creative dramatics, which is a kind of storytelling in action.

Making Inferences

The next step after opening to your imagination is to allow ideas to be extended or elaborated. Anything can suggest several probable or possible associations. Even "two plus two equals four" may evoke memories of a teacher and early school years, or an association to the image of a person oversimplifying an argument.

As with the challenge of learning to listen to the still, small voice, or to see with the mind's eye, the challenge of daring to speculate goes against the habits of thinking that are often inculcated during the school years. Emphasis on fixed systems of information evaluation, such as knowing the correct answer through true or false and multiple-choice questions forces a student to avoid as irrelevant the possibilities, elaborations, and ambiguities in situations. Dwelling on implications or allowing the mind to wander imaginatively creates poor study habits and poor grades. Most guessing activities are discouraged, and great value is invested in repeating specific information. For example, rarely, if ever, are students asked what they think might be the feelings of the people involved in a historical event.

Inferences are clearly speculative, and certainly they should not be confused with facts. Inferences that are confused with reality can be dangerous limitations of consciousness; however, inferences that are clearly recognized as tentative hypotheses are utilized as sources of creativity in the sciences and arts. Unfortunately, this differentiation is often ignored and the skill of speculating is rarely encouraged. The creative mind needs to be open to imaginative ideas and intuitive hunches, and then prepared and willing to pursue these ideas through logical channels. Many professional activities are based on an interesting synthesis of intuition and objective reality-testing: psychology, anthropology, history, agriculture, and science, to name only a few.

The legendary Sherlock Holmes, noted for his logical, deductive powers, actually pictured a variety of scenarios in his mind. His follow-up of these alternatives was the left-brain elaboration of the right brain's intuition. Sir Arthur Conan Doyle, the author of the Holmes mysteries, based the character of Sherlock Holmes on a real person who was a physician and teacher. When Doyle was a medical student at the University of Edinburgh, he studied under Dr. Joseph Bell, who cultivated his abilities at detailed observation and conjecture and applied them to the process of physical diagnosis of patients. Doyle adapted these methods for use by the character of the great detective when he was trying to solve a crime.[4]

Thus, whether in a detective story or beside your door when you arrive home, a pair of unfamiliar muddy shoes is a fact that invites you to make inferences: Who might be the owner? Where is the person who left these shoes? How did the shoes become muddy? Pursuing it further, what was the source of water that turned the earth to mud? What are social-status implications of these shoes? You can spin off several possible scenarios based on your willingness to allow your imagination to suggest images and ideas as part of the process of making inferences.

Warming Up

A basic skill to be developed in the Art of Play is your ability and willingness to plunge ahead as an act of faith. When a child dives into a swimming pool or pedals off on a two-wheeled bicycle, the nature of the courage displayed is the act of continued movement. This is the essence of improvisation, and it cannot be effectively taught in words. Nevertheless, there are several guidelines that are useful as you begin your own process of experimentation.

Moreno pointed out that spontaneity does not emerge full-blown in any situation; it requires a gradual process of physical, emotional, imaginative, and intellectual warm-up. Athletes are generally familiar with this process. Beethoven was known to pace up and down, gesticulating and humming, as a "starter" for his process of composition.

You begin with general and somewhat stereotyped behaviors, becoming acquainted with the rough outlines and parameters of the role. For example, if you are playing a newspaper editor, starting with clichéd actions of sitting at a desk, reading the newspaper, and adjusting your glasses can lead you toward more dramatic issues, such as an encounter with yourself (soliloquy) or another key relationship (co-character). The expressions that reveal the more individualized aspects of your character's personality develop later in the warm-up.

The early phases of warming up also deal with the realities of context. Role-playing, like any engrossing activity, exerts a mild hypnotic effect. Because of this, it's important to establish an emotionally safe environment. Spontaneity is liberated only when anxiety is relatively controlled. The norms of the group must be such that people feel free to experiment, make mistakes, and know the atmosphere will remain supportive. Group cohesion and comfort must be dealt with before attempting any role-playing activity. Exercises are designed to help the participants become comfortable and acquainted with one another. In these warm-ups the group can establish a clear agreement that performances are not going to be judged, because, from the start, everyone is revealing more of themselves than in common forms of social interaction. When all the players are risk-taking, the collective psychosocial energies accumulate; each act "gives permission" to everyone to go further.

Subjective Involvement

Our culture often models communicative behaviors that are indirect, tentative, and distanced from immediate responsibility. People avoid speaking in terms of "gut-level" messages that begin with "I." Rather, they tend to express intellectual opinions; relate events in terms of abstract generalizations; expound narratives in the past tense; and use other indirect forms of speech (e.g. "Don't you think . . . ?" "It would have been better . . ." "One doubts that could have happened," etc.). However, if you engage in serious role-playing, these tendencies must be reversed.

The basic goal is to plunge into your imaginary character, almost as if the events were really happening in the here and now. Therefore, consider the following rules of thumb:

Speak subjectively, as if you are the character: "I . . ."

Speak in the present moment: "I am here . . ." Instead of describing how you would be if you were to play the part, or how you played the part in your mind, play it here and now. Imagine that the surroundings are before your eyes and the events are occurring now.

Speak in emotional terms, describing your likes, dislikes, desires, and fears: "I feel . . ." This brings the character alive far more than explanations.

Respond to your imagined environment. Enjoy or suffer from the experience of the clothing your character is wearing, the qualities of your surroundings in the scene: "Huh, this uniform is getting to be too tight." "Ah, how lovely: the flowers are in bloom."

Begin to dramatize, amplifying the feelings and actions of your character. Dare to soliloquize openly: "I'm pretty successful at this business, you know. It takes not only experience, but a bit of shrewdness just to survive, and I've managed to do better than that. Yes, sometimes I have to bend the law a bit, but business is business."

Speak directly to your co-characters or to the audience: "I'll show you how I interview a prospective employee."

Emphasize your emotions even if your character would ordinarily seem somewhat flat on the surface: "I may seem like a nonentity to most of the world, but when I get together with the band, I play a lot of solos!"

If you're playing a role that ordinarily is not associated with human emotions, play it as if it did experience a human range of feelings: "I am the gate in the dream, made of straw and pearls. I can collapse so easily, yet I am an entrance to a realm of treasure. I beckon you." Or, if you're a part of a body: "I am Stephen's neck, and I'm kinda cramped and tight, but I feel safer that way—sort of ready for action . . ."

Amplify your statements. Don't be satisfied with only one statement about a situation, but go on to add further comments. Let each point lead to another, allowing the inferences to be expressed as an elaboration of your character: "I'm forty, though I don't feel it, even if I am getting some wrinkles. And a few gray hairs. I must admit, though, I've thought more about dying in the last few months than I ever have before."

Move around as much as possible. Gesture, relate to the furniture or other elements of your imagined surroundings. The body gives a great number of physical cues to the mind, which in turn intensifies the warm-up, as well as suggesting new dimensions of your character. Using your voice appropriately to your role also enhances your experience. The more you express yourself in the role, the more you begin to feel the role.

Using Spontaneity as a Stimulus

You'll find you can make use of the props in the room or impulses in your body as devices for developing the action. A piece of cloth, a chair, a stick—all may be woven into the drama, and their unique properties will suggest more ideas to further the action. For example, let's say that you're a character in a scene and find yourself confronted with an imaginary book, but you don't know what the book is about. (Sometimes this type of event happens when exploring a scene from a dream.) Open it, turn the pages, and behave as if you could read it—only that it's a bit blurry. As your actions proceed, you'll begin to get intuitive flashes about the words, or at least the hint of words: "Hmm, it seems to be about some scientific subject . . . but I see that it's really a metaphysical theory . . . there are some intriguing symbols . . ." Similarly, if you sit down as if to dine, you'll be able to sense what foods are on the table or are being served to you. You sniff, breathe in deeply, and say, "Ahh, [fill in your response]!"

Be Sensitive to the Flow

A major aspect of improvisation is a willingness to integrate new information as it arises. If you're playing a role in a certain way and it's not working out, give yourself permission to shift your role. You don't have to impress anyone, nor do you have to be clever enough to think of a smooth resolution. You could simply say, "Wait; I want to play it differently," or, "Stop; may I take that over?" It's important to trust your capacity to correct errors of judgment as you go. This happens many times every minute as you ride a bicycle. It's interesting to note the rockets to the moon were technically off course a major percentage of the time. Even though the error was slight, the plans anticipated that midflight corrections would be necessary.

You may enjoy incorporating a surprising turn of events, such as some spontaneous action by your co-character, an intriguing suggestion by the director, or even a new aspect of your own character that you have just discovered. Indeed, if you're warmed up sufficiently, you'll discover that you can trust your own spontaneity; more often than not, your instinctive responses to an unexpected turn in the action will be excitingly effective in catalyzing the play in a new direction.

Once again, this idea goes against the subtle cultural injunction that you must think before you act. While such a principle is useful for planning the building of a house, there are many activities that go better when spontaneity is allowed to operate more freely. In contexts such as role-playing, forethought becomes counterproductive.

In conclusion, the skill of moving into action in spontaneous enactment involves the cultivation of imagination, warming up, and daring to improvise. The Art of Play invites participants to become receptive to the subtle yet richly dynamic processes of the imagination. Cultivating the rich reservoir of the imagination through activities that develop a sensitivity to creative impulses helps recapture a valuable dimension of being human. Fantasy games, awareness exercises, and the like may serve as useful warm-ups for dramatic practice.[5] These also support the skill and facility of speculating, making inferences, and turning simple facts into potential stories.

Permitting yourself to plunge into improvisation can be helped by reminding yourself that in play there is endless room to make "mistakes." When you're making up a character's identity, you can change anything you like and experiment with new configurations. That's what play *is*. Allow what might otherwise seem like a mistake to become transformed into an opportunity for further creativity: "Well, that approach isn't working. Let's change something." The director and group will support your experimenting with varying some dimension of your character, or even a major shift of role or scene. You can enjoy being a playwright and codirector as well as an actor. Likewise, you use these same principles for warming up to your role as a co-character in someone else's enactment.

The next chapters will address the more complex skills involved in developing a role in depth and applying a variety of techniques for exploring the possibilities of a character. Because they illustrate the rich variety possible in the Art of Play, these issues are important even if you're not yet ready to utilize them.

Chapter 7

ELABORATING ROLES

As you become more skilled at thinking in terms of roles, the challenge arises of deepening your experience in role. In this chapter we will present a number of techniques for getting in touch with some of the more subtle dimensions involved in any role. These are fundamental approaches that can be applied to the technique of role reversal in general, which means they serve as the tools for developing interpersonal sensitivity and empathy in everyday life.

There may be times when you'll want to use your skills simply to express some feelings through exploring a role. If you're with friends in a playful context, you may want to portray a caricatured role, full of clichés, freely stereotyped, or exaggerated with fluff and nonsense. At other times, however, your artistic and psychological integrity will lead you to discover some fairly realistic aspects of a chosen role. The purpose of role creativity is not to ridicule, but rather to bring forth compassion and to touch the inner depths of a role. Thus, whether you're the main character or co-character in an enactment, let your internal guiding focus be to pursue the question, "What would it be like if I were really in this situation?"

Further Considerations

There are a variety of questions to be considered when you're warming up to the nature of a role:

Remember that in role-playing, there are no absolutely correct answers concerning the qualities associated with a role—it's all what you make of it. Thus, if you were a baseball, would you feel the experience of being struck with a bat as pleasant or unpleasant? Some people like it: "I feel as if I were made for that breathtaking moment when I'm hit hard and off I go into the sky!" Others hate the idea: "I prefer to be thrown gently—I don't really like those jarring moments."

What are the advantages and disadvantages? Every role may be thought of as containing a variety of aspects, some of which are experienced as pleasant, others, unpleasant. For example, "I like being rich and famous. I can eat in the best restaurants or I can hire the best cooks and eat at home. On the other hand, I'm constantly being asked for money, as gifts, loans, or crazy investment schemes. I'm also uncomfortable about all the gossip and distortion that goes with fame."

Comparing your role with something in a similar category helps you to sense your advantages and disadvantages. For instance, "I like being a desk lamp because I'm less isolated than a floor lamp; I have more intimate objects sitting next to me at my base— papers, pencils, a coffee cup." Or, here's another example: "One thing I regret about being a Great Dane is that I'm too big a dog to be allowed on people's laps, and I miss what I experienced as a puppy."

Imagine the kinds of events that would evoke emotion. These occur in the course of your experience in role. There are four primary emotions that you can relate to, just as there are primary colors or principal tonal elements in music. These can be diagrammed in a chart, similar to a color wheel:

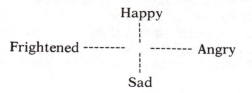

Most feelings are expressions or mixtures of these primary feeling-states. Ask yourself, then, what events could occur in the course of playing your chosen role that would result in your feeling happy?—sad?—angry?—frightened? You can substitute words such as satisfied, regretful, irritated, or worried. When you're in character, these more subtle emotions may be easier to identify with. For example, as a four-year-old, what might frighten you? If you were a famous businesswoman, what would make you happy? If you were a home computer (with feelings), what would irritate you? Also, you can wonder what might lead your character to experiencing the most extreme forms: ecstasy or exultation, furious rage, absolute terror, or the depths of depression. A good starting point, then, to developing your skills for sensing into any role is to ask yourself questions relating to the categories of advantages, disadvantages, and events evoking the four primary feelings.

What are the challenges innate in the role? Every role implies a variety of subroles and suggests some probable future events. This kind of awareness is facilitated by the practice of making inferences, as mentioned in a previous chapter. For instance, the role of being newly married might imply the further challenges of moving away from parents, the decision as to whether or not to have children, and the stresses of creating a joint monetary policy. The role of a fireman might include the anticipation of a new piece of equipment or the worry about cuts in the taxes. Thus, consider the hopes and concerns that are part of a character's situation.

How does the role differ from the cultural norms? Most people are acutely aware of even slight deviations from the social and group ideal of appearance, ability, or behavior. For example, if you are portraying a character who is shorter than the others in his surroundings, build that into your role elaboration. Similarly, if the person is a member of a racial or ethnic minority, the chances are that this variation is part of the person's awareness. This applies for political, age, religious, gender, and other aspects of the character. Even if the difference might be something that you (out of role) would overlook in others, remember people tend to be self-conscious, and these deviations from the ideal may seem significant to the character you're trying to understand.

Include also more subtle deviations, such as a slight accent or dialect in speaking, a lack of college education, or a mild exaggeration of some physical feature. Differences in life-style, income, and values are dependent on the context in which the role is being played, and what might be part of the character's normal social network can become a source of dramatic interaction when they take place in a different subcultural situation.

What can the body language of the role teach you? Various roles have associated characteristic postures, facial expressions, gestures, or some other aspect of nonverbal communication. As you imitate or perform these actions, the internal sensations of the body's muscular and nervous system will give you feedback, clues that evoke ideas about how your character might be feeling. For example, if you play the stereotyped "old lady" who walks in a hunched-over position, that posture will influence other aspects of your behavior and will remind you of some of the bodily concerns of aging.

Experimenting with physical postures and movements is an integral part of learning to deepen your involvement in the many dimensions of a role. Your body can help center and focus your characterization, enabling you to spend less time trying to think about what to do. Practicing different walks, gestures, postures, facial expressions, or tones of voice will help you be familiar with your range of alternatives.

There's a technique in psychodrama called the "double," in which a group member or an assistant therapist helps the protagonist to express their emotions. In learning how to function effectively in this type of role, the person who is the double is instructed to mimic the posture or nonverbal actions of the protagonist. This helps the double to get in touch with the subtle feelings of the person for whom they are doubling. This idea may be extended to the task of warming up to a role in more playful contexts, also—if you take on the actions of the role, some of the feelings follow.

There is a theory in psychology about the nature of emotions that is receiving some renewed attention. The James-Lange theory suggested that it is the body's behavior toward fight, flight, or the expression of other feelings that to a significant extent determine the experience of emotion.[1] Thus, behaving in a depressed fashion increases depression, or tensing your body and acting in a hurried, impatient manner tends to increase your inner sense of irritability. Applying this approach, you can use the cues of the kinesthetic mode to help you develop a role you are portraying or seeking to understand.

Working from the Self-System

Another major technique in role development involves the conscious use of phraseology. The point is to work within your character's "self-system," a term coined by the psychologist, Carl Rogers, to indicate the view of the self and the world from the person's own frame of reference. This is in contrast to the kinds of terminology that are used to describe others, usually involving generalities and psychological jargon. For example, people who are relatively psychologically sophisticated might describe negative qualities in others using terms like "manipulative, hostile, defensive, stubborn, immature, controlling, emotional," and so forth. However, people rarely describe themselves in these words. Furthermore, such terms could be applied to most of us in some stressful situations, because there are some of these characteristics in everyone. Thus, words like "manipulative" are not only tinged with negative judgment, they are also not part of the self-system of those being labeled.

Phrases that would be closer to those typical of the self-system might be more like these: "I just want to make a point." "This is unfair." "You're making me feel like the bad guy." "Why can't they understand me?" People usually present themselves in a manner that tends to justify their position. Sometimes, they offer a self-deprecating facade; however, this is really a subconscious gambit used to deflect real criticism. For example, a person might say, "Well, I don't know anything about this, but I think . . ." or "I don't want to be bossy, but I'm really concerned that you get this right."

To recognize the patterns of words used to develop characterization, or to deepen a role, it's useful to read some of the work in the field of semantics. One particularly helpful idea is found in a book by Hayakawa.[2] He writes how the same quality can be described using different words or phrases that have contrasting emotional colorings or connotations. An amusing exercise in this regard was developed by the mathematician and philosopher, Bertrand Russell, which he called "The Conjugation of an Irregular Verb"—a parody of the terminology used in teaching grammar. The game is to describe a given quality in three forms, each having a different connotation. The first person ("I") always speaks of the quality in a highly complimentary fashion; the second person ("You") is described in a mildly critical or slightly negative form; and the third person ("He," "She," or "They") is/are represented in the most disparaging manner. For example, one might say: "I am intelligent; You are shrewd; He's devious." Or, "I am creatively imaginative; You are a bit scattered; She is crazy." or, "I am philosophical; You are melancholy; They are moping." It's fun to make up your own list.[3]

Some people tend to put themselves down. In their self-systems, they choose the least favorable connotation to describe their own behavior, even to the point of belittling some aspect of themselves that might be considered a virtue in others. For example, they might say, "I know you'll think I'm crazy to say this, but . . ." rather than "I just got a creative idea!" As you can see, they are using the third-person negative forms mentioned in the exercise above to describe themselves. All of this illustrates the plasticity of the experience of reality; you can make of it whatever you want, depending to some extent on the words you use.

Role Conflict

As mentioned in the earlier chapters, roles are themselves multidimensional and contain components that may be in conflict with each other. This is an extension of the advantages and disadvantages concept, but it refers to actual occasions for painful or awkward decisions. For example, there comes a time in the life of most young people living with their parents where the desire to be cared for directly conflicts with desires for independence. Another example is a fireman who might say, "I like being a bit heroic, but sometimes I feel like I have to do things that I know are foolhardy."

Such role conflicts also represent interpersonal issues, as well as being intrapsychic. Thus, a person such as the fireman mentioned above might experience the conflict in terms of the expectations of others (rather than inside himself). In this same way, a school principal might feel, "They want me to be firm, but when it comes to their own kids, they want exceptions to be made."

One way of viewing this involves seeing every role, every person, as being in some ways "caught in the middle." People are pulled between competing demands for loyalty, priorities, values, interests, expectations, and the like. Addressing this phenomenon in playing a role tends to give depth to your character, as well as providing some directions for further enactment. In real life, a helpful way to express support for other people is to acknowledge the dimensions in which they are trying to balance conflicts of interest.

Another way to develop a role is to allow the complexity of a character to become a source for dramatic ideas. Many characters naturally embody several different dimensions, and these may generate conflicts, also. For instance, if you chose to play the role of a young college president, the incongruity of your age could become the focus and catalyst for an encounter with a much older faculty member.

Elaborating Relationships

One of the simplest ways to develop basic skills in roleplaying involves taking on a character and talking about it; however, it becomes a more interesting experience when two people take on roles and interact. Everything we have said about the dynamics possible in one role is thereby expanded. Many of the same techniques may be applied in bringing out the dramatic issues.

Each role relationship has its advantages and disadvantages, aside from those of the characters alone. Thus a father-son encounter contains certain almost universal themes; and these change, depending on the ages of both parties. They would also be different if the younger person in the relationship is a daughter. Adding a third, fourth, or fifth character to a given scene involves the dynamics of alliances, teams, subgroups, and other social psychological phenomena that create good dramatic material.

Playing the Co-Character

In role-playing or sociodramatic enactments, usually one person initiates the basic theme and thereby becomes the main character. Others who volunteer or are chosen to participate become co-characters. Among adults, it's best to have some clarity about how these roles are to be played; for example, the main character may want the co-characters to play in a more or less specific way to create a context within which an experience can be expressed. "I want to be a football coach and I get to boss everyone around." After the group agrees to play this scene, the director's role is to facilitate its enactment. On the other hand, the main character can set up a general role such as, "I am trying to pick up a girl at a nightclub." The director invites volunteers to be in the club and to freely create their roles and styles of play.

Therefore, if you are in the role of the co-character in an enactment, follow the guidance of the director. Enjoy the opportunity to improvise within the structure of someone else's imaginary setting. With or without direction, freely portray whatever aspects of the role seem interesting and/or appropriate. This will either stimulate the main character toward more spontaneity or evoke correction and guidance that can help define your role.

In summary, the process of the Art of Play may be facilitated by the participants' bringing out the subtleties and emotions of the roles they play. This chapter has described a number of ideas to help players elaborate their roles more effectively.

Chapter 8

USING DRAMATIC TECHNIQUES

The activity of developing your role-taking ability is enhanced by knowing a variety of psychodramatic techniques. In this chapter we will discuss the following:

director's commands	behind the back
asides	audience roles
the soliloquy	role reversal
the double	replay

These techniques and others noted elsewhere in the book may be used in the Art of Play when improvising scenes, in order to bring out psychological dimensions that lend depth to the activity. As you read the following material, you might think of a variety of contexts in which you could apply these ideas. For instance, in a supervisory session, in a small group, or among friends, you might be doing some role-playing. Although these psychodramatic methods were originally developed by Moreno for his modified form of group therapy, they can be adapted to situations such as classrooms, personal growth programs, and recreational activities such as those described in this book. As a participant, you can suggest these techniques to the director in order to help you experience your role most meaningfully. If you're the director of a role-playing session, it's useful to know about the following techniques as resources.

Director's Commands

The process of role-playing is one of continual revision. As such, it is an exploration rather than a performance. The players don't try to give polished or smooth portrayals of their characters. Rather, they're allowed—even invited—to pause and reformulate the direction of the enactment. "Is this the way you want it to happen?" will always be the director's implicit or explicit question. Another basic directional attitude is exemplified by the question, "What else would you like to experience in your role?"

This kind of tentative, co-creative process resembles in some ways the earliest phases of a rehearsal of a play, at which time the actors are getting the sense of their characters, the director is trying out alternative approaches to staging, and even the playwright might be revising some lines. (Some people involved in the theater have reported that, for them, this phase of production is the most exciting time.)

The director of a role-playing session may request a pause in the action when it seems appropriate. Perhaps the players need more help in warming up to their characters, or there may be too much or too little conflict or friction in the scene. Any commands may be chosen to stop and restart the action, depending on the preference of the director and the group. The word "Cut!" (taken from the movies), the phrase "Time out," or "Let's pause," can indicate to everyone that the enactment is stopping momentarily. A related command is "Freeze!" which suggests only a very brief or minor revision; the players maintain their physical positions and retain the momentum of their dramatic ideas and feelings until the phrase "Carry on," or "Continue" is spoken.

When the director calls for a pause in the action, there

may be a brief informal conference about what's needed. Sometimes, no discussion occurs, but the director simply suggests one of the other techniques noted at the beginning of the chapter. However, if it is unfamiliar to any of the group members, the director should take a moment to explain its use to make sure everyone knows what's happening.

Anyone in the group can call for a pause in the action, but this should be reserved for occasions when someone is feeling really uncomfortable, rather than simply having a different idea about how to stage or enact the scene. The goal is to allow the director to experience a creative process, also. Group members should stop the action only if someone becomes aware of a fairly important issue that isn't being addressed in the group dynamics.

We recommend that groups have only one director. However, if there are two directors, they need to approach their responsibilities with the same attention co-therapists give to their roles in a group. A codirector can function to keep an eye on the audience and make suggestions regarding the action on stage or the whole group process. The codirector also can assist the director and play roles when necessary.

Asides

The technique of making asides is useful for introducing several levels of information. It is a familiar gimmick in animated cartoons or in an old-fashioned melodrama. For example, the villain in the course of an action may stop suddenly, turn to the audience, hold one hand up to the corner of his mouth, indicating that the other characters on stage cannot hear, and say, "Ha, ha! Little does Nellie know that John Strongheart will never arrive in time to pay the mortgage, because I have drained all the gasoline from his car!" Then he turns back and resumes the action: "Ah, Nellie, my fair beauty . . ."

The aside may also be expressed silently, with a well-timed glance directed at the audience, expressing scorn, disgust, mischief, anticipation, or surprise. The double take is a way to show surprise by looking twice, with one glance at the audience in between.

The Soliloquy

The classic example of a soliloquy is Hamlet's speech in Shakespeare's play, when he reflects in a moment of indecision: "To be, or not to be . . ." The soliloquy is an extension of the aside and occurs, as in Hamlet's case, in that intimate moment shared between the character and the audience, in which he speaks as if he is talking to himself, but actually speaks aloud so the audience can hear also. The soliloquy can occur as the character is portraying a solitary action, such as walking home after work, getting dressed in the morning, or waiting for an important interview. However, it works better if the speaking can be associated with a physical action, which reduces the self-consciousness of the player.

The Double

Another way to bring out the hidden feelings in a role can be achieved with the use of the double. One of the group members positions himself at a slight angle to the main character. This position allows the double to observe and imitate without intruding. It's helpful for the double to mimic the posture and expression of the main character. The director announces, so that players and audience are all aware of the new element in the drama, "Now this is (insert the name of the main character)'s inner self, the emotions you would not ordinarily express in the scene; this part of you will say things aloud, and if they help you to get in touch with your deeper feelings, go ahead and repeat the statements. If your double is not accurately portraying your unspoken thoughts, worries, and so on, then you must correct them."

This technique, as with the use of the aside, allows for the drama to unfold on two simultaneous levels: the spoken and the unspoken. You can imagine the many situations in life where what is thought but not outwardly expressed is really the most dramatic part of a situation. An interaction with an employer, spouse, or parent may be enriched by seeing the hidden confrontations, confessions, and admissions of vulnerability.

If you're the main character, and your double says things that feel out of character to you, be sure to correct them. The double should be trying to enter the mood of the main character, and corrections or suggestions (including those by the director) are important feedback on your progress. In this regard, the main character should validate the double when they are really connecting. When rapport isn't established, the double may be exchanged or dismissed while the action and play continues. It should be noted that this powerful psychodramatic technique is very useful in psychotherapy.[1]

Doubles also may be introduced for the other major co-characters in the scene. Then you will have two levels of dialogue occurring simultaneously. For example, picture this arrangement used by one player as politician welcoming a rival. Effusive praise on the expressed level might be mixed with hostility revealed on the level of the doubles. This technique can create a fairly comical scene when the enactment is lighthearted, or it can add poignancy to dramatic encounters.

Behind the Back

The behind-the-back technique is a variation of the double and asides, in which two or more characters speak openly about another character as if he wasn't present. However, for purposes of dramatic continuity, the character being talked about need not physically leave the room; instead, that player simply turns his back, and this signifies to the audience that he will henceforth act as if he had not heard the conversation. Later in the action, that person reenters the scene and continues whatever process need to happen.

For example, if the scene is in a business office, and the co-characters want to set the scene by engaging in a bit of gossip, the director would turn to the main character and say, "(The name of the character—let's use 'Mary'), you are not in this scene. Please turn your back." Then the director would address the co-characters: "(Their names), in this scene you are talking about Mary before she arrives at work." The other players proceed with their gossip, which is a dramatic way to generate some background information; then, at the director's signal, Mary enters, acting as if she hadn't heard a word of it. This technique helps the co-characters develop their roles and the story while allowing the play to progress without interruption. The dramatic tension can build while at the same time issues and events are created to be explored further.

Audience Roles

Enactments may be enhanced by creative and appropriate participation by the audience. The group may be directed to function like a Greek chorus, repeating or chanting certain phrases as background for an interaction on stage. The audience can be asked to create sound effects. Some scenes require the participation of as many people as choose to join in, such as a circus parade, a flock of animals, or a crowd being addressed by a prophet. Removing the boundary of the proscenium arch, the traditional barrier between audience and actor, is actively utilized in the Art of Play and is built into the structure of psychodrama.

Role Reversal

The technique of role reversal has been called "the heart of psychodrama" because it invites the participants to rise above the role-playing and to encompass in their minds the other roles involved in an interaction. The technique consists of two players exchanging roles. Thus, if Jim as King and Judy as Wizard agree to reverse roles, then Jim portrays the Wizard and Judy, the King. Role reversal is used for several purposes:

To correct another player's portrayal of a role. Thus, a main character playing a husband might say (out of role) to his co-character, "No, that's not the way I see my wife answering: let's change parts and I'll be her." They reverse roles, he shows how she acts, they reverse again, and the scene proceeds from there.

To experience more than one role in a scene. For instance, if you started out being a knight, and one of your co-characters was a dragon, you might get the urge to play the dragon. You could ask the director, "May I switch roles? I want to be the dragon for a while." It it's your enactment, you'll be allowed to play any part you like.

To gain insight into how the other person might be feeling in role. If there is an argument between two characters, they can change parts and become familiar with the other person's point of view. This may be done as standard practice in psychodrama. It is even more effective in real life. It works best when both people are willing to open their minds from a narrow focus and bring their integrity to the challenge of presenting the other person's position as sympathetically as possible. The techniques for getting in touch with the various dimensions of a role (mentioned in the previous chapter) are useful in this endeavor. Usually people involved in this approach discover some basis for acknowledgment of goodwill and valid concern which can lead to negotiation and reconciliation.

The opportunity to reverse roles is a special feature of psychodrama, and when used in imaginative enactment, it can enrich the experience of the participants more than traditional approaches to creative drama. Role-playing as an educational experience is also significantly enhanced by the inclusion of role reversal.

Replay

At the end of an enactment, there are often feelings among the audience members about how they would have liked the scene to be played. We refer not to judgmental reactions, but to various participants' interest in exploring their own versions of aspects of what they've witnessed. Someone then may request to play their idea, or else the director could invite further role exploration: "Would any of you like to play part of the scene *your* way?" One of the audience members,

Mike, might raise his hand. "Yeah, I'd like to be the house-wife, and I want to show how I'd handle the salesman." If all agree, Mike takes on that character and demonstrates or explores how his alternative strategies might be played.

Another form of replay can occur when, in the course of an enactment, there is some impasse. Then, with the consent of the players, the director asks for feedback from the audience/group. For instance, imagine that the main character, Bob, is playing a scene showing conflict with his brothers; he gets stuck, and indicates that he wants some help. The director turns to the group and asks for feedback: "Would anyone like to show Bob how they would cope with this situation?" A few hands shoot up, and the director picks one: "Okay, Sara, come up. You are facing the brother." The action then proceeds until Sara's strategy is clear; then the director dismisses Sara to rejoin the audience and asks the original player if he'd like to try again. A more successful interaction usually follows, and the scene may continue or close with a sense of satisfaction for the main character.

A third variation of replay occurs when the main character is dissatisfied with how they are playing the scene. For example, you might be playing a sheep in a herd and begin to feel uncomfortable. You could say, "Time out. I don't like the way this is going." The director reflects this by asking, "Do you have any ideas how you might want to replay the scene?" "Yes," you answer, "Instead of being compliant, I'd like to be more mischievous." "All right," says the director, "start the scene with your being that way," and the play proceeds.

Some replays can be very brief, rather than involving a whole scene. For instance, if you're the main character playing a teen-aged daughter, you might say, "I want a small replay." The director nods in acknowledgment, and you say to your co-character, "Bill, play my father more aggressively. Give me a harder time. Let's go back to where you tell me I can't go out tonight." The scene moves back to an earlier point in the story and then resumes so that you can refine your portrayal.

Finally, remember that scenes may be replayed to allow

for the fullest satisfaction of the main character's desire to explore a role. Thus, you may wish to practice a behavior repeatedly, in order perhaps to feel the excitement and sense of mastery of a self-assertive skill. In the scene above between a daughter and her father, the person playing the daughter may wish to stand up to the father several times, escalating or varying her actions.

In summary, there are many psychodramatic techniques that can be utilized to deepen and intensify the experience of enactment. Exciting dramas occur when people shift roles, exchange roles, replay scenes, and, when needed, take advantage of the whole range of techniques available. These techniques facilitate and freely use the elements of drama to help create a wide variety of approaches to enactments. Many imaginary and alternative scenarios wouldn't occur in real life, and it's important to remember that psychological dimensions seek expression, too. Using the methods described above, that expression can be fun, valuable, and a shared experience. Further references on techniques are included at the end of this book.

Chapter 9

INTEGRATING OTHER DIMENSIONS OF SPONTANEITY

Children often move easily among a variety of activities when they play. In the same spirit, the Art of Play accommodates the following possibilities:

singing, making music, playing rhythm instruments
dancing, marching, funny and dramatic body movements
all kinds of games, sports, athletics, exploratory play
telling stories, jokes, poems
playing with dolls, hand puppets, toys
wearing costumes, hats, masks, makeup, using props
making flags, drawings, designs

These and related behaviors reflect a wide range of self-expressive vehicles for imagination and spontaneity. There is no real compartmentalization into art or drama or music. The mind of the child can encompass all the arts and all the roles in the theater. Each of the aforementioned activities offers a channel for a special kind of vitality. For example, the experience of singing gives you an involvement in music that is different from any other type of play. The reintegration of all these forms in adult play results in a celebration of the wholeness of the personality.

The first point to be made is that if, in the course of a dramatic enactment, it seems fitting or amusing to break into a song or dance, by all means do so. If a scene invites a parade, have the group members who are being the audience join as co-characters in a burst of exuberance.

The various kinds of activities noted above, then, may be used as part of the process of enactment itself, as part of the warm-up, or as a separate complementary diversion that validates the many dimensions of spontaneity that seek expression in your life.

Music and Singing

Music has special magic. However, what has been said earlier about the cultural inhibitions to dramatic play applies also to explain the reluctance of many people to raise their voices in exuberant song. Contemplate the exultant improvisation of the mockingbird. Remember the joy of sitting around the campfire and singing together. No one cared how well anyone else sang; no one needed accompaniment—everyone sang *a capella*.[1]

A major purpose in cultivating the dimension of song is that it vibrates your chest, heart, and whole body. There is a powerful experience to be had in belting out a song. Many people rarely raise their voices, and this chronic constriction of range also reduces the experience of extremes of emotionality. Yelling in anger or sadness in dramatic or therapeutic settings cannot substitute for the vigor and subtle expressiveness of a variety of songs. Thus, let there be more occasions for really loud singing in your life. (Soft singing and whispering is fun, too.)

Singing, like dramatic play, can only be learned by doing it. Unless you're one of those rare people who can sight-read from music, you will pick up the melody of a song most easily by repeatedly singing along. You'll make lots of mistakes, notice them, and gradually and naturally correct more of them with each repeated rendition.

Notice that trying not to make mistakes doesn't work; if anything, trying too hard makes it more awkward. You can't really hurry the process. Some people pick up songs easily, most people take a bit of time, and a few never seem to get it "just right." It doesn't matter, though, in the world of play. (This process of learning by doing and not trying has many applications beyond that of acquiring the skill of singing. It serves as a metaphor for many kinds of experiential learning, to differentiate it from the "forced feeding" of didactic practices in education.)

It's not necessary to apologize or comment about how you're not very good, because this is a friendly context and such behavior only inhibits others. Making unnecessary excuses communicates that you are very aware of how well you are or are not doing, and others begin to feel you might be equally judgmental of them. Instead, be patient and good-humored about your own imperfections, which opens up the process for everyone else, too. The more you enjoy yourself, the more you'll find you can sing more freely and fully.

When you're experimenting with singing, try out a range of variations:

humming	nasal, with a "twang"
loudness	falsetto, high-pitched
operatic	sexy, breathy
silly	sweetly
Middle-Eastern	mournfully, blues style
jazz, bebop	monster/animal voice

A variation on singing is fooling around with funny mouth sounds, the way you might have done as a child. Snorts, whistles, clicks, the sounds of motors, guns, falling bombs and explosions, all are expressive noises that can be great fun both as an accompaniment to songs and to dramatic enactments.[2]

Another technique is that of singing or speaking in a se-

ries of nonsense syllables. Speaking gobbledygook or gibberish is not so hard, and with some practice it can become more
natural and spontaneous. You can make up your own language, lifting elements from foreign languages that you may
have heard spoken. It's fun to see what comes out.

You can combine singing and this made-up foreign language in order to sing in the style of folksongs, religious rit-
ual, magical incantation, or opera. Certain kinds of melodies
invite improvisation like this, and it's more interesting to fill
in the notes with strings of exotic consonants. The American
jazz tradition has a language form called scat, and it may be
sung to boogie-woogie rhythms, as done so well by singers
like Ella Fitzgerald. It's even woven into the lyrics of such
songs as *It Ain't Necessarily So*, or *Good Morning Star-Shine*.
Phrases such as "Zip-a-dee-doo-dah, zim-bam-boodle-oo, be-
do-bop, skiddoo-dle biddley-bop," and similar bouncy
expressions add spice and rhythm to an exciting melodic
flow.

Gibberish may be integrated into the flow of creative
dramatics, also. Characters may be portrayed who speak a
made-up foreign language, so that fierce expostulations, seductive manipulations, pompous pronouncements, evil in-
timidations, intoxicated ramblings, philosophical musings,
and other styles of speech can be expressed without having
to come up with real dialogue.

Improvising with musical instruments becomes an extension of singing. If one is accomplished, real instruments
such as pianos, guitars, or harmonicas may be used. For most
people, it's easier to play with kazoos, slide-whistles, a variety of percussion instruments, and other simple gadgets.
(There are several cities that have organized kazoo bands to
march in local parades for fun.) It's also a form of play to
convert ordinary objects into makeshift instruments.

To return to the play of singing, this may be integrated
into the Art of Play as a warm-up, a shift to a different activity, or for the closing period, as a form for sharing warmth
and fellowship. As such, it increases group cohesion and re-
laxes everyone. We prefer to use familiar, simple, and uplifting songs, and we hand out song sheets so people don't have

to worry about remembering words. The goal is always to facilitate spontaneity by minimizing concerns for performance. Sometime we'll play the songs on a cassette recorder so that people can feel that they're singing along rather than leading.

Simply expanding the repertoire of songs you know and can sing by yourself has beneficial features. You discover you can express your various moods more eloquently. You have a skill that allows you a pleasant diversion on the road, in the shower or bathtub (or hot tub), and at parties. Exchanging songs with friends can be as personal and valuable as many gifts. Many people have vivid memories of where and from whom they learned a favorite song.

Movement and Dance

Experimenting with some of the nuances of gesture is one way to elaborate a character. This kind of exploratory activity has enjoyable aspects of its own, also. You can make up a kind of combination of dance, mime, and just fooling around as you try out and expand your repertoire of physical actions.[3]

When these are accompanied by music or song, or even in silence, a kind of dancing emerges. If you're not much of a dancer in a particular form, play with your body's movements as a clown might, feeling the style, and consciously exaggerating your lack of expertise. Play with some of the following activities:

funny walks	postures	primitive dance styles
bouncing	leaping	vaudeville struts
staggering	falls	lurching, monster-style
karate, kung fu	gestures	animal movements
facial expressions	dying	various gestures

...and other improvisations.[4]

A related activity, somewhere between singing and moving, is the realm of experimentation with voice tone, inflection, and pacing. Experiment with your voice as you would with body movements. Other sources of movement styles that can serve as ideas for your vocabulary of action include the following:

folk dances	Feldenkrais exercises
ballroom dances	Bioenergetic Therapy
show dancing	Alexander techniques
ballet	flamenco dancing
tap dancing	square dancing

Whether the movements are based on dance or therapy, your repertoire may be extended by learning some of these forms.[5] Practice in these physical behaviors is helpful in reducing the many layers of habit and inhibition we learn as we grow up in this culture.

Drawing and Construction

Simple forms of drawing, painting, doodling, and coloring came naturally to you as a child. You told stories, made simple cartoons and designs, and created funny characters. Your early efforts were expressive rather than representational.[6, 7] The Art of Play includes such activities, because they, too, are channels for spontaneity and vitality.

One example of how this medium may be utilized as an interactive form of play is a technique we have developed and named "draw a mandala." *Mandala* is a Sanskrit word meaning a circular diagram, and it refers to any somewhat symmetrical, circular design.[8] The psychiatrist, Carl Jung, thought that making mandalas had a powerfully integrating effect on the psyche. Working in pairs, one person begins by drawing any size circle on a piece of paper. Then the two people take turns adding to the design. Several colors may be used, and about 10 minutes suffices for people to discover an interesting or amusing result. Variations of this exercise include having the people draw with their nondominant hand, that is, their left hand, if they're righthanded, or having the whole group do one large mandala.

Another general activity for you is to experiment with your own doodles and drawings. You may discover there are certain styles and themes that make up your own personal vocabulary of images. Drawing your own mandalas and geometric designs can serve as a basis for aesthetic improvisation.

In the undifferentiated world of childhood, your dramatic play and artistic activities would overlap. Thus, you might be designing a city area in your sandbox, drawing pictures of cities and buildings with Spider Man or Superman leaping around, and be enacting those dramas when you're with your playmates. Portraying the realm of knights and kings and princesses serves as an occasion for you to draw pictures of heraldic emblems, personal coats-of-arms, pennants, or flags. You can also draw your castles, pictures of your armor and weapons, and maps of your territory. In adventure play you might draw blueprints of James Bond's 007 supercars or the layout of some exotic hideout.

Doodling may also be applied to the creation of secret codes, exotic alphabets from made-up languages, and other forms of imaginative play involving the processes of writing itself.

Another discovery that can come from playing with drawing is to find you can create characters through your doodling, the way so many cartoonists do. The popularity of Kilroy at the end of World War II revealed an indigenous inclination to cartoon, resonating with a growing enjoyment of the world of comics as an art form.[9] Play with it and make up your own little creatures.

The contemporary interest in unicorns, wizards, dragons, Smurfs, Snoopy, and other fads reflects a pervasive desire for self-expression in the realms of imagination, and for personal symbols that communicate this mythic urge. Creating your own characters can give life to imaginary playmates, elves, monsters, heroes, and other magical characters in your fantasy.

If you want to warm up to this activity, consider the range of characters generated by the world of storytellers, cartoonists, and comedians. Who would you add to this list of people we've particularly enjoyed?

Mel Brooks	Al Capp	Jim Henson (The Muppets)
Jonathan Winters	Walt Disney	J.R.R. Tolkien
Jackie Gleason	Saul Steinberg	Ursula K. Le Guin
Carol Burnett	B. Kliban	Shel Silverstein
Red Skelton	A.A. Milne	Lewis Carroll
Gary Larson	Lily Tomlin	Peter Sellers
Ernie Kovacs	Bill Cosby	Beatrix Potter

The construction of masks, costumes, hats, and environments (i.e. scenes, clubhouses, decorating the playroom, building forts, etc.) all are extensions of the creative imagination. They are also media for the development of your own personal symbols. Just as some primitive tribesmen would express individuality and originality as they improvise upon a general design for bodypaint or hairstyle for various ceremonial occasions, so you can experiment with face painting (a recent fashion at neighborhood carnivals), costume, and the like.[10] You can elaborate these by adding magical swords, wands, or other objects and props that can amplify the power of a costume.

Toys and Things

You're never too old to play with toys. "The difference between men and boys is in the price of their toys".[11] Although our culture tends to generate increasingly expensive and complex gadgets, don't forget the fun you had with construction sets, stuffed animals, and other favorite toys of your childhood. Allow yourself to enter the world of your children's playroom, and to act as if the various dolls, cars, and other toys were alive. Pens can become rocket ships, screws or acorns may be lined up as if they were soldiers, and other makeshift articles may become the source for imaginative drama.

Hand puppets are a particularly useful toy that may be used even more productively by adults. Often they are ambiguous enough to take on a variety of possible interpretations. They invite discovering the voice that goes with them, and so they function as excellent warm-ups for later character enactments. Using hand puppets is also an enjoyable way for people to meet and begin to interact.

In improvisational dramatic activities such as the Art of Play, props may be used as a good warm-up. Something like a stick, chair, blanket, hat, or card table may be placed in the middle of the room, and group members take turns making the prop into something that goes with a character. For example, a stick can be used as a cane, a flute, a baton, a rifle, etc.

The range of play is limitless. Allow your activities to become integrated, so the dramatic, artistic, poetic, and dance-related experiences become vehicles for the fullest expressions of your vitality and imagination. Consider also the possibilities of climbing, playing with clay or dough, sand, food, and cooking together, juggling, and all the other components of play that could potentially be used as part of dramatic play. Your inner child has the capacity for being a mime, playwright, artist, dancer, director, actor, sculptor, storyteller, cartoonist, and all the other creative roles that serve to celebrate your individuality. If you look for these parts of yourself, they will begin to emerge with energy and delight, to the greater enhancement of fun in your own life and that of those around you.

Chapter 10

THE INHIBITION OF PLAY

Discovering playfulness in actual experience is a rich and enjoyable activity; however, you'll encounter occasional deterrents as you begin to explore the Art of Play and talk with others about the realms of spontaneity and imagination. We think it's helpful to be aware of the psychological dynamics that fuel the resistances, the better to overcome them. The resistances may be in your own mind, or words murmured by friends and family that echo attitudes in our culture that tend to inhibit the expression of playfulness. Some of the following phrases might sound familiar to you:

> It's silly. It's ridiculous. That's just for children. You don't even know what you're doing. It's crazy. It's weird. Don't be a show-off. You're just boring everyone. You can't do it, so don't try. You'll just make a fool of yourself.

Part of the challenge of the Art of Play is learning to modify these beliefs, for even though they may be only minor, such attitudes can inhibit your spontaneity. Here's an exercise that will warm you up to the kinds of issues we'll be discussing. You may find you can answer the following questions better by sharing them with some friends and talking about the memories:

> Recall the time in your childhood when your make-believe play occupied more time than any other mode of play. When did this change, and what were some of the factors effecting the change?
>
> When did you play with dolls and stuffed toys? When did you stop?
>
> Did any adults play imaginatively with you? Who were they?
>
> Who did you know who modeled playfulness in an older age group?
>
> At what age were you taught about games that involve winning or losing?
>
> For how long were you able to sing, color, or draw expressively without any concern about whether you were doing it correctly?
>
> In your family, neighborhood, or school, what happened when you made a mistake while playing?
>
> What special talents, skills, handicaps, or other qualities helped or hindered you in your social play?
>
> Did you have enough playmates, or were you somewhat isolated, by reason of location or restrictions?
>
> Were you able to find a group in school or in your neighborhood who shared your age, abilities, interests, values, and/or temperament?
>
> Were there many traumatic experiences in your childhood, such as being bullied, isolated from a clique, teased, or dominated? Who was there to help and protect you? What residual effects have these events left?
>
> What was play like with your family members? What kind of jokes did you like, and still like? What was the

role of humor in your childhood? How often did you laugh?[1]

What experiences in your school, church, or clubs helped or inhibited your spontaneity?

Having thought about these questions in your own life, you'll be better prepared to understand the issues that follow.

The Prevalence of the Problem

We believe a number of psychological and cultural problems derive at least in part from distortions in the experience of play in childhood and adolescence. Among these are:

The tendency toward addiction or fixation on a narrow range of sources of gratification (discussed in Chapter 14)

The prevalence of shyness and discomfort in group settings

The reluctance to experiment with singing, drawing, dance, and playful dramatic behavior

Awkwardness around others who are being more playful

Not knowing how to play with young children; feeling envious or irritated even with well-behaved but exuberant children

Some forms of vague and generalized mild depression

Restriction of play to competitive or structured activities

We will examine the various factors that inhibit playfulness in the next three chapters. We'll review issues of individual and cultural resistances to spontaneity, the discomfort with fantasy, competitiveness, etc. To begin with, however, we address a primary psychological phenomenon.

Repression—The Primary Defense

Repression is a term describing the mental maneuver of doubly denying an uncomfortable feeling and/or thought; sometimes this will include associated ideas or memories. The specific issues are buried, so to speak, and the mind goes on conveniently to "forget" they exist.[2] Repression requires a form of self-deception in which the mind tells itself to compartmentalize unwanted emotions, files them away, and forgets where they are. This process is an immature way of handling unhappy experiences and occurs as part of growing up. Most adults continue unconsciously to use this residual, rather primitive defense mechanism unless they have learned to work out their feelings in more effective ways (e.g., through psychotherapy or other programs of personal growth).

A more mature defense mechanism is called "suppression," and, in contrast to repression, it involves a conscious act of putting aside certain uncomfortable feelings or thoughts. The maintenance of some awareness of the act thus allows the person to deal with the emotions or ideas at a future time, perhaps when more support or strength is available. When repression is used, the mind cannot easily gain conscious access to the issues involved.

Because of the primitive operation involved in repression, the experience of the emotions tends to be stronger. Indeed, the emotional components contain some of the unmodulated quality experienced by a young child or a person under severe stress. The very intensity of the process of pushing thoughts and feelings out of awareness generates associated anxiety whenever they threaten to come into consciousness. Although mature people in a supportive setting can learn to cope with and work through their repressed issues, the initial experience is somewhat frightening, as if allowing the issues into awareness poses an overwhelming threat.

Repression also operates in an overgeneralized fashion. In burying feelings, major associated memories and thoughts are also thrown in. Not infrequently, this includes some valuable needs and aspects of psychological functioning. For example, it's quite common for people to have repressed themes (things they consider unacceptable) from the following list:

anger	not caring, being apathetic
receiving presents	being ignorant of anything
making mistakes	spiritual inclinations
being silly	wanting attention
independent thought	wanting to be touched, caressed
being messy, dirty	being vulnerable, needy
loneliness	being out of control
emotionalism	parapsychological experience
having qualities reserved for the opposite gender	

Any item on this list can find expression in a socially acceptable way or in a distorted, destructive, or neurotic form. Indeed, when they have been repressed and subjected to an immature process contaminated by anger at the self and others, their initial expression is often in the less socialized form. Furthermore, if important parts of the psyche are repressed and build up enough, and are never allowed a conscious expression, they'll frequently be manifested as neurosis, psychosomatic illness, troublesome character traits, or other problematic behavior. It is interesting to note that some of the secondary defense mechanisms resulting from repression take the form of symbolic activities opposite to the original needs. One example is people who maintain a very serious attitude because they're afraid their more playful feelings will be detected and ridiculed by others. However, once a repressed dimension becomes conscious, it can be worked with, utilizing the healthier parts of the mind. The support and encouragement of others during the process can help a person find more positive expressions.

A curious feature of repression is that it simply does not work well enough. The true nature of the mind is an integral whole, and an attempt at self-deception cannot be sustained, especially if important emotional needs are being repressed. These needs are always seeking some expression, and so they leak out. Then, in order to maintain the repression, whatever thought or feeling has tempted this escape, or has acted as a reminder of the repressed and anxiety-laden ideas, must then also be repressed. This causes a spread in the range of experiences that must be avoided. As a result, the kinds of roles that are comfortably engaged in must become more constricted. Repression requires psychological energy to not think about what's naturally trying to come to mind. All of this can leave someone feeling tired or drained, which adds to the person's loss of vitality.

There are many differences among the various theories of dynamic psychology, and yet all agree that repression operates in the general manner described above. The disagreements tend to be about which of the various emotional needs in the psyche are primary. We address this last point in a more inclusive and holistic fashion by our theory of role dynamics described in Chapter 1.

"Naughtiness" and Playfulness

One of the challenges in finding effective channels for the needs and psychological functions listed above is developing a level of discrimination as to what's acceptable and what's excessive. The degree to which parents have repressed any of these issues significantly affects their children's capacity to deal with these dimensions of personality. If the parents are having trouble with their own repressed material, the children may be inhibited or distort their own expressions. Unfortunately, sometimes parents unconsciously indulge and even subtly encourage antisocial behavior which reflects their own repressed needs.

The process by which children discover the realistic limits of socially acceptable behavior is what we call "naughtiness." It is a normal and healthy way of exploring the intangible world of social expectations and requirements. We're not referring to clearly hurtful or malicious kinds of behavior, but rather the relatively innocent realms of giggling mischief. For example, recall the glee of young children knocking down their buildings of toy blocks. There's a catharsis of pleasure as they discover the capacity to destroy what they've built. Recognizing the socially constructive and approved nature of building, they also sense the paradoxically delicious discovery of the good feelings associated with the "badness" of causing the blocks to fall and scatter. Similarly, there's a secret awareness of the fun involved in saying naughty words or looking at things that are off-limits, according to social mores.

Included in this early form of testing the limits of reality are many categories such as excretion, sex, defiance, aggression, religion, lying, respect for authority, and even language. Children not only discover the limits dictated by social convention and family rules, but, more importantly, discover the flexibility of these limits. As we adults know, there are a wide variety of ways to circumvent the rules. Children learn these and delight in disguising the expression of the ideas, being secretive, and playing tricks. The fun of playing with the many kinds of naughtiness becomes a major activity in childhood, serving the need to manipulate activities related to rules and taboos.

Repression of the "Inner Child"

Adults remember on some level of consciousness their own capacity for naughtiness. If they've had to repress ideas and feelings associated with those earlier playful explorations, then these repressed complexes are manifested in a variety of ways. As mentioned before, one way is simply to avoid play and make fun of or reproach anyone else who enjoys playfulness. Another variation is to compartmentalize and devalue play by categorizing it as "childish." This scorn is applied to anyone beyond mid-childhood who continues to indulge in playful behavior. "Foolish," "silly," "being stupid," and other terms may be used, but they all refer to an implicit attitude that anything smacking of the exuberance of early childhood is not appropriate in the teenage years or adulthood.

When people repress feeling or thoughts that have to do with basic needs, they lose touch with valuable, associated sources of vitality. For instance, the repression of vulnerability can inhibit the expression of sensitivity. When the need for attention and support is drastically devalued, a person may reject the dimension of caring about relationships. The complexes of repressed material include important qualities such as innocence, exuberance, imaginativeness, and spontaneity, as well as residual, immature tendencies to whine, sulk, or tease. For the adult, all these elements together may be called the "inner child." This term roughly corresponds to Eric Berne's description of the "child" ego state in his system of Transactional Analysis. The healthy goal is to able to accept the whole inner child, learning to channel and temper the less socially acceptable impulses.

People might try to "prove" they are not a child by engaging in behaviors that are the opposite of what is associated with anything childlike or playful. This reinforces the process of repression through the use of a secondary defense mechanism called "reaction formation." Some of the ways this may be done include: being overly serious, irritable, belligerent, tough, callous, inappropriately nonchalant, self-righteously devoted to work or to some cause, chronically mildly depressed, etc.

An unfortunate consequence of adults' repression of their inner child occurs when they pass it along to their children, or pupils, if they are teachers. When children play, it reminds many adults of their own repressed feelings, and the accompanying sense of being threatened, mentioned earlier, can get converted into behaviors that ignore, avoid, or actively suppress children's spontaneity. Children sense their parents' anxiety, and often choose to repress their own playfulness, rather than risk losing the closeness of the relationship. In this way the pattern may be passed through a series of generations.

Parents may overgeneralize when stopping a child's play, implying that it's the desire for play itself which is the problem rather than the more likely issue of the child's poor timing. Whether busy with household tasks, preoccupied with other matters, or simply tired, too often parents may refuse an invitation to play by reproaching (e.g., "Stop bothering me! Why are you playing instead of doing your chores?"). This type of communication can lead children to devalue their own play. It would be preferable to validate the child's needs and then say no simply (e.g., "That's nice that you want to play, but not now.")

Play is also devalued because it represents a loss of control. Repressed people tend to generalize their fears so that any spontaneous and exuberant activity provokes a need to contain and subjugate it. This confusion of "childlike" and "childish" has led to rationalizations of patronization and exploitation of preindustrial cultures, women, and other groups. Fears of loss of control on a collective level are expressed as needs for unquestioning respect for tradition and authority. The element of naughtiness in play is sensed as a challenge to social conventions, and so societies based on repression tend to be less tolerant of playfulness.

Actually, play is an excellent way to learn healthy self-control without repression. The mechanism used in this process is called sublimation. It is characterized by symbolic activities that serve to generally satisfy an impulse. In other words, enacting a need or desire in a social context increases consciousness about its motivational roots and also creates or sets up a situation for learning acceptable forms for its expression. This results in people growing up with a sense of access to a full range of emotional potentialities, with a role repertoire flexible and broad enough to serve them as situations arise.

Envy and Hostility Toward Childhood

Even as play for repressed people symbolizes a threat to loss of control and the possible escape of naughty feelings or thoughts, it also represents the unconsciously longed-for freedom to express the wholeness of the spontaneous self. Thus, adults who have repressed their inner child feel they were forced into doing so and resent the loss it entailed. In turn, they envy and resent anyone else who seems to have escaped this fate. Unconscious envy is manifested in our culture in a variety of pervasive and subtle forms of hostility toward the natural playfulness and vitality of children.

Many adults who consciously love or even just like children nevertheless may harbor some unconscious feelings of envy, hostility, and associated defense mechanisms in proportion to the degree they (unconsciously) believe themselves restricted from enjoying life as much as it seems children do. Furthermore, these dynamics may become elaborated into irrational behaviors, including an unconscious form of sadism.

While the term sadism may seem harsh, the dynamics involved are essentially similar to those more fully elaborated in the sexual perversion with the same name. For some adults, the inner child represents a weak but threatening part of the psyche, and therefore it requires periodic symbolic defeats by the forces of self-control. This internal drama attempts to protect the conscious self from awareness of the anxiety-provoking thoughts and feelings that are being repressed. The mind thus symbolically "proves" to itself that it can master these inner forces that threaten to break through into consciousness, and enjoys the sense of power and superiority that accompanies this victory. Unfortunately, the drama is all too often played out in relationships, and particularly in behaviors involving children.

Even when the sadism involved in the mistreatment of children is subtle, it nevertheless involves a denial of the children's real needs and feelings as they become externalized figures of the repressed adults' internal drama. Two other defense mechanisms are utilized to disguise this behavior—projection and rationalization. The inner child, when repressed, is experienced as somewhat rebellious because of its natural force for self-expression. In addition, the sense of internal conflict associated with repression contaminates whatever feelings are repressed with anger. The nature of the child is then sensed as potentially destructive, although this view is essentially a projection of the adult's distorted inner child. The negative feelings are further justified by rationalizing them, which fosters child-rearing systems emphasizing the role of training and control.

A relevant example of this complex of unconscious envy, hostility, sadism, projection, and rationalization was the phenomenon of overconcern about "spoiling" infants in America and parts of Europe in the late nineteenth and early twentieth centuries. The idea was very fashionable and frequently propounded by physicians and educators. The prevalent belief about spoiling was not coincidentally associated with a number of other ascetic, late Victorian traditions.

The whole issue of spoiling was overgeneralized, so that giving a child pleasure and attention, even in infancy, was considered dangerous. The truth is that it's not possible to spoil a child with pleasure and attention up to the age of about two or two-and-a-half. Nevertheless, in the atmosphere of overconcern generated by many repressed adults who were unconsciously afraid of their own inner child, parents were cautioned against expressing affection, feeding on demand, and almost any other indulgence or response to the child's needs. This included discouraging behaviors that were obviously aimed at seeking attention. Any attempts by the child to negotiate alternatives were redefined as "just trying to get his own way," and therefore deserving of refusal for that reason alone. It was important that the child learn "who was the boss." Although the conscious belief was that such an approach to child rearing was an effective way to build strength of character and self-discipline, it was used most often as a rationalization for plainly sadistic motivations on the part of the adult.

Alertness to the idea of spoiling has some merit within certain limits. Children between the ages of three and six need to discover they can master a variety of skills in spite of their frustrations. They need encouragement to sustain their efforts. On the other hand, overprotectiveness will lead to a sense of self-doubt, associated with a tendency toward being overly dependent, pseudo-prideful, and an attitude of entitlement—in other words, spoiled. Other neurotic and characterologic disorders can follow, and these dynamics were described in detail by Adler.

Another example of the unconsciously hostile bias toward childhood may be found in Freud's choice of the Greek legend of Oedipus to describe a complex of behaviors observable in children around the ages of four through seven. He termed "the Oedipus complex" children's irrational jealousies and conflicts regarding their sexuality and their parents. His theory, reflecting his culture's beliefs at the turn of the century, placed the onus of destructive impulses on the child.

Although there is some truth to Freud's observations, further studies revealed that an important contributing factor to these issues developing into problems in children was the degree to which the parents engaged in behavior reflecting their own emotional needs and repressions. In healthy families, children work through these issues naturally in the course of their imaginative play. The ironic (and revealing) feature of the Oedipus legend is that Oedipus's father, Laius, consciously attempted to murder his son on two separate occasions, while Oedipus himself acted in ignorance. Thus, it is worth considering that this complex could also be used as a way of illustrating the unconscious hostility toward children rather than vice versa.[3]

Unfortunately, at times, the complexes of repression of the inner child, envy and hostility towards children by adults, are expressed as overt sadism. In contemporary society this is observable in the dynamics of child abuse. In the child-rearing practices of the nineteenth century, it was seen most flagrantly in the customs of what today would be considered excessive corporal punishment. Beyond the overt infliction of pain, a variety of insults, name-calling, and impositions of onerous tasks on children continue to be widespread examples of the externalization of repressed issues.

It should be noted that cruelty is not necessarily part of human nature. Gentler approaches to child rearing have shown that children who are treated well, and played with, tend to become naturally empathic—they instinctively imagine themselves in the other person's role. Under the pressures of abuse, however, and considering the way too many children in Western culture were treated until the middle of this century, this openness is reversed, resulting in insensitivity or actual cruelty becoming the dominant behavior. This is because children raised in an environment of physical and/or emotional subjugation need to symbolically reassure themselves that they are powerful by demonstrating that it is the other people who are weak (i.e., the defense mechanism called "identification with the aggressor").

This neurotic need for dominance results in a wide variety of behavior problems in children, and the patterns of devious manipulation may continue into adult life.[4] Another example of how these patterns can be externalized and expressed on a cultural level has been the widespread lag in recognizing the emotional and physical needs not only of children, but of any group whose lack of power generates a sense of guilt and reactive hostility. This partially explains the cultural lag in dealing affirmatively with the needs of women, the aged, the poor, the handicapped, and other disadvantaged groups.[5]

The Lack of Appropriate Models

Where can you find models for imaginative, spontaneous playfulness? Bill Cosby's family program currently on television is an example of both playfulness and constructive problem solving, but it is a rare exception. The characterizations of some actors and comedians attest to the enjoyable potentials in playing a wide variety of roles. If you were particularly fortunate, you may have had someone in your family who communicated the zest for drama in life and the richness of its enjoyment—perhaps someone with qualities like Mary Poppins, Auntie Mame, or Zorba the Greek. It would suffice if someone sang songs or played imaginative games with you and your siblings.

Unfortunately, in our discussions with people, we find that many have had no one who modeled the joy of being a grownup. It's hard under those circumstances to see the payoff in taking on the responsibilities of adulthood, and we suspect that this may be a significant factor in promoting the avoidance of the challenge by so many disturbed adolescents. Even an enthusiastic, warm, and slightly "nutty" teacher or camp counselor could serve as an effective and refreshing alternative to the conventional range of adult behaviors.

The English language itself seems to have no terms that communicate the intrinsic health and value of playfulness. As mentioned before, words like "crazy" are applied to dramatic behavior that's not officially sanctioned by a clown's makeup, a costume, or being on stage. Even if the term "crazy" is used with an affectionate chuckle, it is a misleading association. Intentional playfulness, effectively and appropriately expressed in social contexts, is actually extremely difficult for mentally ill people.

The present terminology in the field of dynamic psychology further undermines the nature of imaginative enjoyment. One term for a type of sexual perversion is exhibitionism, but this is also a term that describes dramatically expressive behavior. A phrase used to describe play is "regression in the service of the ego," but the choice of "regression" implies a retreat from adulthood, rather than a celebration of integration. "Acting out" is yet another descriptive term used both in a general and a specific sense. Both usages tend to imply an unconscious neurotic mechanism rather than a conscious choice of symbolic expression.[6] Thus, even the psychological system lacks descriptive names with a positive connotation for imaginative activities, and this makes it difficult to recognize and validate the healthy functions of self-expression and make-believe.[7]

Models for the available range of play in our culture tend to be dominated by popular games and sports based on competition and performance. However, there are other cultures who engage in more cooperative games.[8] By introducing the idea of the fun to be had in playing together toward a shared goal, adapted forms of these approaches, along with activities such as "New Games," can function as models in educational and recreational programs.

For many people, having fun raises the image of lying around, hanging out, getting drunk, goofing off, or generally engaging in nonconstructive behavior, if not downright antisocial activities. A major problem in our culture is the present structure of education and work, both of which are compulsory and often boring. For many people today, fun is anything associated with escape from those situations. If you think about it, however, the escapist kind of fun wears thin after awhile. This needs to be countered with more options for constructive fun, activities in which the enjoyment is proportional to the involvement, creativity, social cooperation, and achievement.

Cultural Factors Inhibiting Play

Repression can function on a collective level as well as an individual level. Indeed, many cultural taboos and traditions are sustained by people simply never daring to even think about alternatives. This seems to be reasonably effective in societies that are fairly stable, but in times of significant change, the mental inflexibility associated with rigid beliefs can be maladaptive.

Anthropologists note that cultures tend to foster those qualities in children that are most compatible with the requirements of the socioeconomic structures, religious beliefs, and other traditions. However, there are often cultural lags, so that child rearing and educational practices tend to continue to address the development of abilities that are more appropriate to an earlier social milieu. This phenomenon is more marked in situations (such as our own culture) where there has been significant social and technological change.

Western society is gradually emerging from several centuries in which seriousness, hard physical labor, unquestioning respect for authority and tradition, and a degree of asceticism were virtues. Playfulness, imagination, and spontaneity had little place in the mainstream of socioeconomic processes, and so were correspondingly devalued. However, as we are rapidly evolving out of the industrial age and into a postindustrial, electronic age, the changes in technology result in a reversal of the qualities that are most adaptive. More specifically, the shift from farm and factory to computers, services, and other "information-intensive" activities invite people to be creative rather than blindly obedient, questioning rather than accepting, able to discover relevant patterns rather than limited by habits of rote memorization. Rigid relationships in a hierarchical social structure are no longer as effective as flexible, voluntary organizations, such as networking systems and self-help groups.[9]

Not only is our technology evolving, but the increasing interchange with other cultures that this makes possible leads in turn to a shift in attitude from self-righteous ethnocentricity to a more open-minded capacity for understanding and dynamic relationships. Thus, another difference between industrial and postindustrial cultures regarding the most adaptive abilities would be a corresponding shift from arguing/debating or oppressing/rebelling to negotiating.[10]

In summary, the qualities needed for healthy functioning and growth of individuals and the culture include flexibility of mind, initiative, inventiveness, and social effectiveness. These are directly promoted by the experiential learning that occurs in improvisatory dramatic play. Play allows the mind to operate at some distance from the task, because it uses the category of "not really real" as a kind of laboratory for trying out different possibilities. There is a distance between the actor and the observer, a distance that fosters an ability to consider alternatives beyond the conventional modes of thought. In nonserious states of mind, the unconscious dimension can be allowed to bring its creative potential to bear on a task, and the ensuing flashes of insight or intuitive hunches often lead to constructive solutions. Accessing these resources in the human psyche requires a freedom from repression that can be cultivated in children and adults through active involvement in appropriate, spontaneous playfulness.

Chapter 11

REALITY AND FANTASY

In addition to the social and personal resistances to playfulness and spontaneity, there is also an intellectual tradition that rationalizes the need to perceive reality in simplistic terms. The realm of fantasy play creates a sense of pervasive discomfort in people who are particularly attached to the security of clearly defined systems. Three specific examples of this process of rationalization will be investigated:

Play is not realistic, and therefore somehow an avoidance of life.

Indulgence in fantasy play can lead to mental illness.

Make-believe is inauthentic and phony.

These misunderstandings are based on some very common but mistaken or limited attitudes. It is hoped a critique of these resistances will help to free you and your friends as you take the risks of rediscovering this fascinating activity.

Dualistic Thinking

People have tended to think in terms of easily understood categories, and these take the form of opposing polarities. One aspect of a category may come to be perceived as exclusive, so that if one thing is true, the other cannot also be true. Some of these include:

good/bad	truth/falsehood
light/dark	science/mysticism
male/female	body/mind
work/play	civilized/primitive
adult/childish	conscious/unconscious
serious/foolish	heredity/environment
strength/weakness	reality/unreality

However, it is becoming increasingly clear, with our growing awareness of cultural relativity, that things are rarely reducible to a dualistic simplicity. The vast majority of situations reveal mixtures of qualities, shades of gray, and aspects that don't fit into any neat system of evaluation. It is important to recognize the many subtle ways in which dualistic thinking oversimplifies and thereby constricts the creative potential of any approach to understanding a situation. Yet such patterns of thought continue to be taught at home, in schools, churches, businesses, and throughout the society.

The dualistic attitude has some of its historical roots in the evolution of religious systems that claimed exclusive truth and righteousness. For the most part, these have been part of the Western tradition; in Eastern cultures, it's possible to be a spiritually active and devout person who practices elements of several religious belief systems. In the history of Western civilization, politics and theology were often mixed, and power could be garnered as each sect attempted to achieve dominance by claiming divine support and accusing everyone else of being heretical, sinful, and/or evil. This occurred whether the group represented a dominant majority or a persecuted minority.

During the Middle Ages, the total domination of Western culture by a monolithic religious establishment tended to create a pervasive intellectual climate in which every action was evaluated as being righteous or sinful. There was little room for experimenting with ideas or activities such as imaginative play. Playful activities fell into the status of vague disrepute. The scientific revolution further confused purposeful fantasy with superstition. Science was engaged in a battle against ideas based solely on the authority of a tradition of opinions, rather than observed and tested fact. Later, the movement of positivism and materialism in scientific philosophy further denigrated the validity of subjective experience.

The Reality of Subjective Experience

The antithesis to a positivist position was the emergence of that school of philosophy and psychology called phenomenology, which accorded a status of reality and significance to what is experienced in consciousness. One practical application of this approach supports that what you feel, dream, hope, imagine, and pretend has a validity deserving to be acknowledged and elaborated in your work and play.

Even though people in Western culture may put great value on the rational, logical, or objective dimensions, in truth, the vast majority of psychological time and energy is spent in the realm of the imagination. Here are a few examples:

hopes	beliefs	stories
memories	intuitions	aesthetic experiences
worries	jokes	sentimentality
style	daydreams	inner dialogue[1],[2]

Even our language, the chief instrument of consciousness, is a product of the fluid process of cultural and social consensus, rather than being something fixed and objectively real. For example, in some other languages, what might be considered universal concepts such as time or number are experienced and described in ways that have no equivalents in English.[3] The experience in the psyche is also a kind of truth, a psychological truth, that may be much more important in a person's life than the objective reality "out there."

Play deals with the realm of psychological reality in which your preconceptions can distort your perceptions. For example, how you feel about something others might consider a relatively insignificant event can trigger a major shift of mood or behavioral reaction. Moreno called his method of psychodrama the "Theater of Truth" because what could be enacted on the stage—the hopes, fears, unspoken words, incompleted acts—all represented a deeper, more personal type of reality.

In psychodrama, people portray not only scenes that have happened in their lives, but more importantly, they also enact scenes of events that have never happened, or could never happen in ordinary reality. For example, a person could encounter and talk with a baby that was never born or say good-bye to a dead parent when one never had the chance. Whether in the Theater of Truth or the Art of Play, you can create a scene from an imagined "perfect" childhood, you can replay a confrontation with a supervisor and create a more satisfactory resolution, or you can conclude an unfinished dream.[4]

There is now a growing acceptance of the validity of personal psychological phenomena. Thus, if someone overvalues being "realistic," you can reply that play encompasses the reality of subjective experience, the reality of consciousness itself. Physical existence is only one kind of reality. Moreover, when you manipulate elements in the realm of the imagination, you are actually opening up crystallized patterns of preconceptions to allow new and more flexible constellations of ideas to form.

Fantasy, Reality, and Mental Stability

Indulging in fantasy or make-believe activities can activate an uneasiness that these behaviors will strengthen infantile patterns of thought and foster tendencies to escape from life. For the most part, this is an unwarranted fear, and untrue. Admittedly, if a person uses fantasy as a way to avoid responsibility, it can be counterproductive; however, when people want to avoid responsibility, whatever way they choose becomes distorted by their self-deceptive intent. The way to differentiate between healthy and unhealthy uses of fantasy and play is by looking at the way it's done. Unhealthy indulgence in fantasy is more habitual, repetitious, stereotyped (i.e., involving only a limited number of themes), partially unconscious, and occurs in relative social isolation.

Sometimes fantasy has been popularly associated with mental illness, and caricatured as a blissful alternative reality in which the patient could dwell happily if tolerated by others. However, the sobering reality is that the true fantasy world of the mentally ill is an arena of endless anxiety-provoking thoughts and images. Being victimized by imagined scenarios and beings is the opposite of choosing to play make-believe characters. Patients who pretend will often not admit it, if indeed they are even aware of pretending. Their reality-testing as to what is make-believe and what is objectively real becomes impaired. Reality-testing is that mental operation which is a major component of what is considered mental health; it consists of checking out your perceptions with the evidence and, to some extent, including in the process the social consensus.

In contrast to deviant behavior or mental illness, imaginative play engaged in for recreation has very different characteristics. The fantasy elements are varied, voluntary, clearly identified as pretending, and open to modification by playmates. In other words, it's a social process, and the player is continuously reality-testing the appropriate contents of the play and relating it to the context.

It's interesting to note that the activity of dramatic play can actually strengthen your ability for reality-testing. The more you pretend on purpose, the more you begin to notice aspects of your life in which you had been pretending unconsciously. In turn, these islands of self-deception become absorbed into a psyche which is generally expanding its role repertoire. Obviously, this has implications for the treatment of certain kinds of psychological problems. The more patients in therapy participate in codirecting, as well as acting in their own dramatic scenes, the more they discover their capacity to be creators rather than victims of their minds and lives.

Authenticity versus Phoniness

In a way similar to how constructive and destructive forms of fantasizing get mixed together, creative role-playing has been confused with compulsive role-playing. Originally, "role" referred to the rolled-up manuscripts used in the ancient theater. From this, the word evolved to refer to the portrayal of any fixed character, with the words and actions generally memorized and rehearsed. Actors who habitually presented themselves in a stylized fashion sometimes tended to "lose themselves" in their role-playing, but it was the **losing themselves** rather than the role-playing that was the problem.

In the 1950s the social roles in our culture were being increasingly questioned, especially by the young people. Hypocrisy regarding sexual mores, self-assurance, knowledge, and other forms of social deception was being identified as "phony." People who developed conscious or unconscious patterns of self-presentation designed to impress, intimidate, seduce, appease, or otherwise gain an advantage were seen as being involved in a kind of "role-playing," in the sense that their real feelings were not congruous with their outward behavior.

By the 1960s, several books were published that addressed the pervasiveness of interpersonal manipulation. One of these, Eric Berne's *Games People Play*, contained many excellent ideas, but the unfortunate choice of words gave the impression that there was something wrong with "playing" and "games." No differentiation was made in the public's mind between conscious, explicit, socially mutual play and indirect, devious, socially exploitative interactions.[5]

In sociology, role-playing was frequently described as if the roles were fixed. However, Moreno, one of the early and innovative role theorists, emphasized the potential of role-taking as a creative and flexible act. Not only can taking on a role be compatible with authenticity, but the degree of spontaneity brought to a role can make its performance a real expression of honest self-disclosure and individuality. In sociodramatic forms of role-playing, then, the participants are engaged in behaviors aimed at heightening authenticity—the opposite of being phony. The play of each role becomes an ongoing improvisation, free of any need to impress or please the audience.

Another aspect of the resistance to play involves the devaluation of imagination as a process. Mary Watkins, in her excellent book, *Invisible Guests*, critiques the tradition in developmental and dynamic psychology which considers imagination to be a primitive or derivative function relative to the centrality of cognition.[6] Disagreeing with this bias, she presents a reasoned argument for reaffirming the place of the conscious use of imagination (especially in the form of imaginal dialogue) in psychotherapy and everyday life.

Thus, we have critiqued those resistances toward play that identify it as unrealistic, escapist, and inauthentic. It is our experience that what is closer to the truth could be stated: Imaginative enactment is a form of recreation that functions to increase one's involvement in the total spectrum of reality, including the reality of the psyche—feelings, beliefs, motivations, all the rest.[7] These may be expressed and explored symbolically, yet consciously, in a social context of interaction serving to enhance responsibility and honest communication. Habitual, manipulative role-playing is the opposite of constructive, intentional playing with roles in sociodramatic, spontaneous, and mutually supportive settings.

Chapter 12

PLAY'S VULNERABILITY TO JUDGMENT

The last group of resistances to play that we'll discuss occur in cultural attitudes that generate a vulnerability to judgment. These take five major forms:

The fear of making mistakes
The contamination of play by hostility or power
The need to justify actions
Competition as a corruption of play
Comparisons

What these various themes have in common is an extension of patterns of dualistic thinking mentioned in the previous chapter. If the person's sense of identity becomes overly focused on being "good" and not "bad," it is a small step to becoming obsessed with being "better than" and trying to be "good enough." The ironic truth is that the majority of behaviors in real life are neutral, neither worthy of praise nor blame. Play contains a preponderance of activities that exist in this realm of indeterminate value.

Unfortunately, it is still quite common for people to be

raised so that they become addicted to praise. In this unhealthy state they are driven by insecurity and live almost
constantly in low-grade anxiety about being vulnerable to
blame. In such a frame of mind, the freedom of imagination
is transformed into a realm fraught with the potential for
making mistakes. Contrast this to the innocence of healthy
development in which actions are relatively free of being
judged or inhibited by expectations of judgment. This freedom from judgment is at the core of adults' nostalgia for the
carefree times of childhood.

The Impact of the Phrase, "Do It Right!"

Early experiences with expressive activities at home and
school often are the roots of tendencies toward perfectionism, performance anxiety, stagefright, and shyness. As an example, consider the way young children are often introduced
to the potentially joyful activity of drawing and painting. Although this is changing, many children have experienced art
activities in a manner that clearly stifles their spontaneity.
Of course, in the Western educational tradition, training the
child tends to be valued more than fostering the natural
processes of development. But whether at school or home, a
child may be told a picture has been drawn incorrectly:
"That's not right, your sun is the wrong color." "This cat has
too many legs." "Fill in the sky." The sensitive child often
feels shame at being corrected this way. A rebellious child
might venture an explanation such as, "But this sun has the
measles!" "That shows the cat is running," or even, "I don't
care about the sky." Such responses are probably considered
disrespectful "back talk" and punished accordingly.

Let's also remember at this point the actual nature of
children's art is primarily symbolic; they make no real attempt to have the stick figures and diagrams approximate the
real world.[1] Some slightly older children do become interested in developing the skill of accurate representation in
their drawing, but this consists of a related but distinctly
different activity from expressive art.[2]

When the activities of singing, climbing, running, dancing, and other forms of spontaneous expression are considered, efforts at correction often result in an inhibition of interest and involvement. These experiences are easily generalized to include the realm of dramatic play. Thus, unstructured activities may be gradually replaced by games with clear rules and criteria for "winning." For an anxiety-laden child, highly structured activities help reduce the vague sense of endless opportunities for failure.

The use of nonconstructive forms of punishment has added to an increase in the overall sense of children's insecurity. Books on training pets emphasize that punishing an animal after the fact is ineffective, because the animal makes no clear connection between its behavior and the action of disapproval. This is equally true in human relations. Children frequently don't know why they're being punished. Furthermore, successfully to correct the disapproved behavior, it's often necessary to show them what else they could do instead.

Many other examples of inefficient child-rearing practices could be noted; but the point is that traumatic experiences tend to inhibit or distort the capacity for spontaneous, imaginative enactment. For instance, children who have been subtly or grossly abused, psychologically or physically, may compensate for their feelings of helplessness by being cruel to other, usually smaller, children. This corruption of play is often reinforced by unhealthy modeling on the part of grownups.

Hostile Play

Children are frequently subjected to teasing. It is a primitive way for someone to feel superior at the expense of another's self-esteem. The victim's righteous anger is usually deflected and even turned back by disqualifying maneuvers such as: "Aw, I'm just kidding." "Can't you take a joke?" "Come on, be a good sport." What the child needs to be able to answer, but rarely knows the words or has the courage to say is, "Well, if that's what you call play, it's not a nice kind of play, and I'm leaving if you don't change!" Teasing, and learning how to stop it, is an issue for adults as well.

Our culture tends to be vague in differentiating between friendly and hostile play, and children have difficulty learning the skills needed to create more pleasant play experiences. Compounding this is the lack of healthy models for exuberant yet loving forms of playfulness among adults; however, this seems to be changing for the better.

Another contamination of the realm of play arises out of the hostility and cruelty of other children. Children who are themselves humiliated tend to pass it along. The pressures of competitive games often become occasions for razzing anyone who makes a mistake. Children with less muscular coordination, poor eyesight or hearing, or more fearfulness often make more errors during team games, and as a result they become subjected to name-calling, ridicule, and ostracism. In unsupervised play situations, this may escalate to acts of clear sadism.

The result of all this is that play as an activity too often becomes associated with feelings of shame and vulnerability—it's a kind of behavioral conditioning. Therefore, it takes a good deal of courage to unlearn the patterns and rediscover that play can be designed to maximize support and eliminate most of the hostile elements. Although a little teasing and mild hostile tension remains in most forms of play, these can often be easily sublimated and expressed in a role. Enactments involving witches, villains, and tyrants achieve their vitality from hostile emotions.

Competition

A certain amount of competition is a common and generally healthy element in play. The problem in our culture is the excessive and, in some contexts, almost exclusive involvement with competitive activities. Little time, recognition, or opportunities remain for noncompetitive forms of play that offer vigorous exercise, teamwork, and challenge.[3]

The pattern for most people begins in childhood with a premature introduction to "zero-sum" games (i.e., a term from game theory that describes situations in which for one person to win, the others must lose; this contrasts with games in which everyone can experience winning). Before the age of seven or eight, it is natural for many children to experience feelings of humiliation and outrage when they are told they lost a game. They simply have little understanding of why games are structured that way.

Often adults or older children who play competitive games with much younger children rationalize their own winning by saying they're teaching the less able child about the "real world." There's only a shred of truth to this statement because, on a deeper level, the most frequent result of losing to others who are clearly superior is a repeated sense of resentful inferiority. For every child who decides to strive harder in an effort to compensate (which is the obvious goal for this kind of motivation), there are at least as many who develop inhibitions or other distortions of both the experiences of competence and the capacity for play.

Compounding all of this is the element of coercion involved in getting children to play competitive games. A child's *choosing* to compete in selected games is an entirely different experience, associated with a free choice of time, place, handicap, and playmates. Competition itself is not necessarily harmful, but competition should not be imposed on children as their only option for recreation in a school, club, or camp. Unhappy experiences with competitive play lead to a reluctance to engage in other forms of play also.[4, 5]

The Need for Justification

A unique quality of imaginative play is that it eludes definition or judgment. If you're playing with blocks, it would be superfluous for someone to come along and tell you you're not doing it right. The obvious answer is that you're just playing. In unstructured play, you can't do it wrong, in an ordinary sense. On the other hand, you never do it right, either—it's an exploratory activity, and thus evaluation by any conventional system is irrelevant. People who have been conditioned to respond to and fear judgment may shy away from such an inherently ambiguous process.

A significant inhibition of playful experimentation comes

from the common interpersonal tendency to demand verbal justification or explanation of behavior. If your parents didn't like something you did, they might have been indirect in their condemnation by asking, "Why did you do that?" or "What's the matter with you?" Adults may think they are being "fair" by offering children an opportunity to present a defense; actually, such a communication only confuses and increases the discomfort of the child. This kind of question-asking can be a subtle form of sadism: "Why did you forget to take out the garbage?" The child might wish to reply, "Please don't ask me 'why.' Just tell me what you want or get on with the punishment. Don't make me testify against myself. I don't know what to answer, and it feels like torture!" Of course, children don't have this level of eloquence, and even if they did, many parents would only retaliate for the "backtalk."

The result is that children who are "put on the spot" a lot may begin to avoid behavior that cannot be easily explained or justified. Imaginative play is a category of activity that might be excluded because of its essential ambiguity. If you're on the defensive, it's hard to feel that any role-playing or fantasy you express won't be attacked as being foolish, silly, aggressive, unacceptable, or naughty. Furthermore, it's unnecessary to explain why you might have chosen to play an airplane instead of a submarine, or any other behaviors. Most of what we do is a matter of habit, spontaneity, carelessness, or is unconsciously motivated, and ultimately impossible to explain. Therefore, people who have been subjected to manipulation through verbal scrutiny often have residual inhibitions of their capacity for spontaneous images and actions.

Comparisons

The final resistance to dramatic play we'll discuss is another culturally pervasive tendency to make comparisons. It's really just another aspect of being conditioned to the dualties of praise and blame, as well as the domain of competition. For many people, it's not sufficient to be better, they must be the *best*. Being second-best is associated with a clear sense of disappointment and a vague feeling of self-reproach (or reproach by someone else whose opinion is valued) for a lack of effort.

It's important to recognize that such attitudes are very destructive to mental and physical health. "Just do the best you can" may seem like an innocuous statement, but it's actually quite confusing, if you think about it. There are no guidelines for knowing how much effort is required to fulfill the injunction. The ambiguity regarding the kinds and amount of aggressive effort that should be expended in any given task in order to be acknowledged as adequate is a primary source of stress in our culture. *How much is enough?*

When this pressure to be "the best you can" is paired with the experience of being reared in a system of praise and blame, it can be very traumatic. Often the praise and blame is aimed at the child, rather than at the behavior: "You're a good (bad) boy," rather than "When you do that, I like it(don't like it)." The result is confusion and anxiety regarding how to retain status as being good or better than a sibling or schoolmates—or at least not "bad."

Worries about this problematical ideal can lead to a subtle form of addiction to praise, manifested by perfectionism, or to a variety of other manipulative character styles. It also provokes chronic anger and cruelty to others, because an insecure child can feel better by making someone else appear worse. Unfortunately, this pattern often carries through to adulthood, and remains a major source of interpersonal or psychosomatic disharmony.[6]

Another way comparisons inhibit play is through the corruption of the expressive arts toward a focus on concerns for status and power. Our culture's competitive tendencies generate specialization even in areas that really belong to everyone: singing, dancing, drawing, and dramatic play, which are natural channels of personal vitality, physical and aesthetic enrichment.

Yet, tragically, how often have children been given the life-negating message, "You're not good enough," or, "If you can't do it well, don't do it at all." The practice of emphasizing recitals, shows, school performances, and other activities prepared for an audience reinforces the selection of "stars," the stress of rehearsals, dependence on scripts, elaborate productions, and a general obeisance to the authority of a potentially critical audience.

In place of all this, an educational approach needs to evolve that offers all children opportunities for spontaneous and expressive activities. Emphasis should be on the experience itself, for the benefit of only those who are participating. The growth of creative drama in the curriculum is an example of this recognition by educators, and it is being extended for use in academic subjects as well.

There is an economic factor that perpetuates the problem—the commercialization of play, both of games and expressive arts. Money in these areas is made only by highly skilled practitioners, supported by large audiences. The problem with this system is that it tends to inhibit the involvement of those who are less talented or determined. Often, what is required for success is a willingness to undergo major degrees of pain or injury, economic exploitation, and a host of other disadvantages; yet, those who aren't willing to pay these prices don't get recognition. Our schools and social institutions have a real opportunity and obligation to develop more programs that offer everyone access to play in a wide variety of areas, without a pressure to become highly skilled.

Thinking in terms of comparisons is further heightened by technology which magnifies both performance and celebrity status of the more successful specialists. The intensification of professional performances is effected by the choice of subject matter and manner of presentation. Emotions are manipulated through the loudness of music, exaggeration of visual imagery, and overemphasis on themes of sex, power, deceit, violence, and individualism in the movies, romantic fiction, and television drama. Costumes, tricks of lighting, makeup, sophisticated sound technology, staging, professional scriptwriters, back-up talent, and the "hype" of the media all create an illusion so removed from ordinary reality that the grass-roots activities of the majority of people engaging in arts or sports play might seem puny by comparison. However, the deep value and vitality of these activities occurs when they become personally relevant. Celebrating the "star" within you and your friends is really what it's all about.[7]

As more people begin to delight in the benefits of playfulness, a movement toward the re-owning of each person's authority to be creative will help shift the culture from a mistaken focus on the product, or what Moreno called the "cultural conserve." It's more important to validate and cultivate the experience of enjoying the creative act itself. Beyond any judgments, each person deserves the right to access all the sources of psychic energy that can enhance the development and expansion of consciousness.

Chapter 13

APPLYING SOCIODRAMATIC METHODS IN EDUCATION

The psychosocial benefits of spontaneity and imagination can also be utilized for more serious tasks. The principles and techniques of exploring situations in greater depth in order to amplify and extend the experiential learning are applicable to such activities as role playing and creative dramatics in the classroom.

Conventional dramatic activities consisting of scripted and rehearsed performances have long been a part of the educational curriculum. Improvisational dramatic work for the purpose of generating more holistic learning related to a subject area is a more recent phenomenon. Although Winifred Ward introduced creative dramatics in Illinois schools in the 1920s, and Peter Slade, Brian Way, Dorothy Heathcote, and others pioneered child drama in Great Britain in the 1950s, these approaches are becoming more widely accepted only since the late 1970s.

Another approach, role-playing, is a related teaching method.[1, 2] A derivative of Moreno's psychodrama, role-playing is widely used in education from preschool to professional graduate programs. Whether for the simulations in

astronaut training or the more personal enactments of problematic situations in nursing or business schools, the experiential mode allows people to find solutions that fit their own
personal styles. Role-playing has many applications, especially in the teaching of social studies.[3] Through enactment,
participants move beyond "knowing about"—the kind of information that can be communicated by books or lectures—
and begin to "understand," which involves the active integration of the imaginative and emotional dimensions of the
mind.

Optimal learning requires more than mere enactment,
however. The dramatic techniques for elaborating roles,
bringing out the deeper and often unspoken ideas, and
changing parts with others in the situation, all help the students rigorously to explore the relevant issues in a situation.
The relatively playful context helps support and motivate
participants to exercise a broader range of their resources so
that these activities should be considered a core component
of genuine learning.

Learning by Doing

Emphasizing the elements of experiential education offers more opportunities to assimilate skills that require a
mastery of their performance. Also, the chance to express
one's own personal style in an activity increases both individual exposure in the group and the sense of belonging. To
some extent, this approach tends to allow students to work
at (and discover) their own pace. Inherent in the principles
emphasized in this book is support for increased use of cooperative rather than competitive methods in the educational process, at least to effect a balance.

In addition to allowing for more practice, role-playing or
sociodramatic enactments utilize the benefits of modeling by
both the teacher and the other students. These components
are similar to the kinds of qualities which foster creativity in
childhood, as noted in Chapter 3. Because of their need for
group process, experiential approaches make the classroom
vital and relevant. No doubt the burden of basic information

delivery will be increasingly assigned to self-reinforcing, student-paced computerized systems.

Personal home computers (and computers in the school) offer a much more personalized experience with information than is possible in most lectures, books, or classroom reviews. Furthermore, educational computer programs allow information acquisition to progress with interactive response features designed to monitor mastery of the material. In the future this could possibly become the way homework is handled as well as being part of special classes during a portion of the school day.

This scenario would enable a fuller utilization of the rich social resources of the school and offer an opportunity for the classroom to flower as an experiential laboratory. The integration, manipulation, and extension of information happens most naturally in real-life situations that call upon the students' knowledge in order to solve problems, make inferences, and create alternative strategies. The classroom offers a perfect arena for students to develop understanding through actively testing and exploring their new skills using role-playing, creative dramatics, and other experiential forms. Through this approach the areas of personal contacts with others, emotional support and challenge, and power of group dynamics expand the potential for multilevel learning. In schools, students can explore and develop abilities that involve the functioning of the whole person.

The educational system is recognizing the growing need for competence in skills of management, research planning, human services, community organization, and other fields requiring more than purely intellectual and technical expertise. In a group-dynamics oriented classroom, the teacher would be oriented toward facilitating the learning of skills in clear communications, interpersonal sensitivity, and imaginative problem solving. These kinds of abilities are best developed through experiential practice with some didactic coaching. Furthermore, such activities involve making the most of individual talents and preferences, and so the recognition of the temperamental and ability differences in students would be fostered.

Sociometry

Moreno's vision for the world is still relevant today: Instead of simply having to adjust to their society, people will some day be able to help change the social structure so that it meets the needs of all the people. One way to do this is systematically to have the people in a social system be questioned regarding their preferences and then sharing the feedback with the group as a whole; then decisions may be made about role distribution and the makeup of teams based on the information. "Sociometry" is the name Moreno gave to his method of using questionnaires to assess preferences in a group. Using this approach, he worked with a number of groups to diagram the implicit interpersonal interactions. These were put on a chart for all to see. It is most important to note that he used his psychodramtic techniques to help the group work through the results of this procedure. Sociologists use sociometry as a diagnostic instrument; however, Moreno's hope that everyone would begin to apply it in all areas of social organization has not yet been fulfilled.

One of the principles of sociometry is that people who naturally prefer to be with each other tend to work more effectively together. It's an approach that encourages teamwork and recognizes the power of social influence. Imagine how your educational experience might have been different if you had been encouraged (rather than discouraged) to sit next to people whom you liked and who liked you, even if you didn't know them very well. Think of the laboratory partners that were assigned; might you have been more successful if you could have chosen each other?

Another observation based on sociometry is that there may be many natural subgroups in a large group. Schools could apply this fact by actively promoting a broader variety of options for activities so that children could discover which kind of people they relate to most naturally. Too often, popularity is restricted to young people with a certain group of qualities, and relatively introverted or artistic children may feel excluded. If only a few major activities are given undue attention or status, it may create a relatively one-dimensional spectrum of those who are "in" and those who are "out." More programs with recognition for talents other than the most obvious (i.e., sports, school politics, performing activities, etc.) could help more children to discover they belong somewhere. Lacking more wholesome options, young people may become discouraged and seek their social role in antisocial or drug-related behaviors. Again we want to emphasize the real need for more noncompetitive activities, because young people need to develop without undue pressures to perform.

The sociodramatic play of children generates natural sociometric choice-making because they get feedback about who they do or do not connect with. As they grow older, it becomes more difficult to obtain accurate feedback, and cliques and shifting alliances generate patterns of indirectness and also outright deception. If there were more group processes used in school, children might suffer less because they wouldn't try to belong to a group that didn't fit their abilities or interests. Also, if some rejections were based on misunderstandings or disabilities, the group could be helped to consciously make some efforts to be inclusive.

Thus, understanding and applying the principles of sociometry would help educators and those who manage organizations to apply natural propensities of people to form alliances as an aid to motivation. Offering opportunities for imaginative play increases chances for interaction and the participants can make more informed sociometric choices. It's like chemistry—the elements must be mixed (and often heated a bit) before they generate the compounds that reflect their innate affinities.[3, 4]

Empathic Understanding

One of the major benefits of experiential education that integrates sociodramatic methods occurs as students learn to understand others by role-reversing and really imagining what it's like to be operating within the constraints of the other person's world. The tendency negatively to judge another person's values or behavior, or artificially to idealize them, can be moderated by having the student imagine both the advantages and disadvantages of the other's positions.

The study of history could shift from a memorization of details to explorations of "what it was like to be." One profitable focus for this approach is to imagine being in ignorance of some things we now take for granted— what it was like to lack some technologies that today seem like elementary requirements for living. Not only can a greater appreciation of the past be developed through this more personal involvement, but, more importantly, students are readied for the future. One of the most important lessons of history is that we continue to be imbedded in the process, and within our lifetimes the younger generation will be viewing the older generations as "history".[5] In other words, it helps young people and the society to help them to dare to dream, to wonder, "What in my world will be old-fashioned a hundred or a thousand years from now?" This exercise should go far beyond the simplistic obsession with nihilistic ideations and entertain the challenging decisions and issues to be faced as individuals, families, communities, a nation, and the global community. Endless opportunities abound for extrapolating past and current information in service of the exciting activity of playing possible future scenarios.

Social studies can use role reversal to become more sensitive to the realities of situations involving:

the handicapped	minorities	underdeveloped nations
primitive people	other cultures	government bureaucracy
authority figures	other religions	younger and older people
small businesses	members of the opposite sex	

For example, a class in social studies or history could have students prepare presentations on "What It's Like to Be . . . " some figures from the past, present, or future. The focus would be on basic experiences, sensations, hopes, fears, challenges, beliefs, losses, triumphs, as they engage in a few events or activities. The material would only cover what the characters being portrayed would be expected to know.

The presentation of unfamiliar political or philosophical positions, alternative life-styles, and the ideals of artists and other visionaries could enable students to clarify and consciously deal with the abundance of new ideas that are coming through the media. The classroom could become a place where students were challenged to develop their own opinions, rather than succumbing to the influences of fashion or blind suppression.

Human Relations Training

The need to deal with sex, friendship, smoking, drinking, drugs, television addiction, excessive dieting, suicide, and other issues is becoming so urgent that it deserves a vehicle than can facilitate the explorations of the topics, yet within the realistic limitations of time. Open discussion is certainly better than avoidance of the topics, but this kind of activity tends to be inefficient, limited to sharing opinions. A much better approach to these emotional issues is through role-playing, or, to be more specific, through sociodrama. The goal of these sessions would be to clarify and bring out many dimensions of the problems, rather than searching for solutions.

Older adolescents and adults would benefit from participation in sociodramatic explorations of future life transitions such as:

marriage	moving
employment	having children (or not)
parenting	aging of parents
divorce	vocational choice and change
retirement	death of friends or family members
sexual problems	chronic illness

Such topics and others could be dealt with in self-help groups, continuing education courses, conferences, spiritual retreats, and many other contexts.

In the development of skills for management, counseling, sales, consulting, and psychotherapy, the uses of sociodrama and role-playing are already valuable tools. Sociodrama helps the participants understand the emotional needs and subtleties of interactions, while role-playing offers opportunities to try out constructive strategies, refine and practice skills. Using role reversal, those in "helping" roles can become more aware of the impact of their own repertoire of behaviors on clients or coworkers, and then go on to learn what actions or kinds of statements are likely to confuse, mystify, or subtly humiliate. "Helpers" who role-reverse with someone seeking their help (or being offered help without wanting it) can have a chance to discover which behaviors are supportive and effective.

Repeated practice of role reversal in professionally relevant enactments has a meaningful place in the training of physicians, teachers, psychologists, nurses, social workers, and others in the helping professions. Empathy is a skill that can only be learned by practice. Intellectual and technical treatment of empathy in books can only offer guidelines and frameworks for thinking about people and their problems. Too often, professional psychology books stress the more severe forms of mental illness, while the typical needs of most patients involve the challenges of how to cope with their everyday problems. The more subtle issues attendant on the vast majority of psychological difficulties remains a neglected part of the curriculum. Role reversal and role-playing are outstanding methods for teaching and learning about how to address problems with clinical relevance.

The actual practice of role reversal develops in the student or professional in continuing education an increasing ability to think in ways closer to the patient's "self-system," a term introduced by Carl Rogers. That is, instead of using the terminology of pathological diagnoses and other forms of jargon, simple, emotionally expressive phrases are used that reflect sympathy for the patient's position. Diagnostic labels can communicate a reductionist attitude, whereas people are complex in the individual choices and expressions of their lives. Being open and willing to enter someone else's reality is an active form of practicing the Golden Rule, or the kind of authentic "I-Thou" relationship described by Martin Buber.

Although role reversal is a method which refers to an act of genuine, compassionate willingness to engage in another's experience, it is more than mere technique. The way to develop the skill of empathy is essentially the same as warming up to any role, which we described in the second section of the book. You ask yourself, "What's it like to be the other person in terms of one of their roles?" Then you ask the same question regarding another role dimension of that person. You go on to add as many roles as you're aware of, and then consider how these various roles interact.

A User-Friendly Language

Another advantage of applying role-playing approaches in education is that the language of role theory, which is used to teach the methods, offers a simplified and unifying bridge to psychology, sociology, anthropology, dramatics, and other fields of study. This language is user-friendly (to borrow computer jargon); that is, its terminology is relatively easy and has many correlations with ordinary speech. Talking about situations in terms of imbalance of roles, unrealistic expectations about a role, avoidance of a role, role transitions, and other themes are expressions that can explain many issues relatively simply. In addition, these concepts can be naturally taught in the activity of imaginative and creative dramatics.

Education as a Core Process

Life itself may be conceptualized as a long series of role transitions, involving a continuing process of unlearning familiar roles, learning new ones, and relearning to use parts of yourself that had been neglected, such as your playful imagination. In this sense, education is a fundamental life process that transcends any system of schools or social institutions. The chapter of this book relating to psychotherapy rests on a core concept that the dynamic, unfolding spirit of life is an educational phenomenon, on both an individual and societal level.

Effective responses and solutions to future developments on this planet will probably depend on human beings acquiring mastery in the basic skills of improvisation, problem solving, creative thinking, and utilizing resources both human (i.e., teachers, consultants, coworkers, etc.), and informational (i.e., sophisticated computer systems). From these skills strategies can emerge for dealing with challenges of "over-choice," overstimulation, population pressures, rising expectations, the impact of new values from other societies and life-styles, dilution of traditional values, propaganda from many sources in the media, social alienation, and an ever changing list of other issues.

In summary, play in education can offer a vehicle for learning the component elements of creativity, initiative, and interpersonal effectiveness.[6] This type of education addresses the need for skills in human interactions. It requires the active participation of the imagination and emotional responsiveness of the students which information alone cannot achieve.

Chapter 14

SPONTANEITY, PLAYFULNESS, AND PSYCHOTHERAPY

Along with sociodramatic techniques, the subject of playfulness itself has an important place in a truly holistic program of psychotherapy. The dimension of spontaneous self-expression is one of the healthiest parts of the personality, and its neglect alone can create an imbalance in the ecology of the psyche. In other words, it's important to have fun.

R. D. Laing, the noted English psychiatrist and family therapist wrote a poem on this topic[1]:

They are not having fun.
I can't have fun if they don't.
If I get them to have fun,
    then I can have fun with them.
Getting them to have fun is not fun.
    It is hard work.
I might get fun out of finding out why they're not.
I'm not supposed to get fun out of working out
    why they're not.

But there is even some fun in pretending to them that
I'm not having fun finding out why they're not . . .
(p. 2)

Although this is a perceptive passage, it also reveals a common limitation in psychotherapy. In attempting to create an atmosphere of sympathy for the genuine suffering of patients, the realm of fun is often ignored or avoided. A grave, concerned expression on the therapist's face may be appropriate at some points in the work, but if it becomes habitual it tends to suggest that the problem is more insoluble than it is. This, in turn, creates an undue dependency on the part of the patient who comes to rely on the therapist's indications of when things have improved.

Another misleading feature of focusing on the problem to the exclusion of the other healthier parts of the patients' lives is that it may perpetuate the "illness." If the patients begin to focus excessively on "solving the problem," they may neglect cultivating several other dimensions of their lives that would be able to help compensate for the weaknesses. Our theory of role dynamics emphasizes the variety of simultaneous channels of personal development, and from this perspective a person may be "sick" in some roles and "healthy" in others. This allows for a better diagnosis of the problems than that provided by dualistic thinking. For example, there are any number of variables which can be problematical in psychological disturbances, such as nutrition, social network, variety of interests, range of strengths and abilities, etc. Difficulties might occur in only a few or in several dimensions. Other areas may be continuing to function quite well.

As an analogy, the psyche can be likened to a garden with the different plants and sections representing the various aspects of the personality. One garden might have good drainage, nutritionally rich soil, and adequate exposure to sunlight. Yet its vigorous and varied plants have become overgrown and infested with insects. This could represent a person who has many areas of strength, even in the face of major conflicts or stresses. With some pruning and cleaning it can flourish again.

In contrast, imagine a garden with hard, dry, and infertile soil, poor lighting, and old, sparse plants. Even if it has no insects and has been weeded meticulously, its general level of vigor is poor. It requires far more work involving general conditioning of the soil and replanting the kinds of vegetation that would do well in shady lighting. In psychological terms, this could describe a person who has few strengths with which to compensate for the stress of life. There would need to be a development of a variety of resources for psychological and social vitality, and this is where the adjunctive aspects of therapy are needed.

Strengthening the healthy parts of the personality is as important as focusing on the person's problems. An important part of the work in therapy can be strengthening the repertoire of roles in a person's life that provide activities for expansiveness and fun. Without remembering the joys in life, there are few real motivations for responsible action. Life-enhancing issues such as nutrition, spirituality or philosophy of life, exercise, and recreation are often neglected as people sink into despair and demoralization. They lose touch with what they like about themselves and forget that anyone else could like them either. Working together to strengthen the overall personality helps a person escape from this debilitating vortex. Furthermore, the theme of playfulness softens the task of therapy, and reminds patients that they are not expected to work continuously on their problems in a direct fashion. Taking time to experience more pleasurable activities becomes identified with a valid healing approach.

Play as a Goal

Learning to have more fun can be discussed as one of the goals of psychotherapy at the very outset of the process. If the patient has fun in ways that are self-defeating, as through alcoholism or delinquency, then the goals of the therapist and patient can include emphasizing the theme of searching for truly enjoyable alternatives. If the patient is unable to have fun, then creating this as one of the goals generates a touchstone for the ongoing process.

Discussing the theme of play allows for the introduction of psychodramatic or action techniques. Resistance to fantasy or dramatic encounters may be lessened when there have been discussions about how pretending and being serious can occur in the same context. This issue should be addressed in a straightforward manner at the beginning of therapy. A natural bridge can be shown by relating use of the psychological device of the "if" dimension when considering the possibilities of various aspects of a problem. The same "if" dimension is also the essence of play.

The role of humor and playfulness in the healing process has become increasingly recognized in the last several years. The approach described above sets the stage for judicious modeling by the therapist and encouragement to the patient for breaking out of the sick role and engaging in playful behaviors that might at first seem incongruous with the state of being in psychological pain.

Play as Part of Personal History

Inquiring about the patient's experiences with play and sources of recreational satisfaction, both past and present, offers an immeasurably rich vein of relevant material for discussion. First of all, the number and scope of enjoyable activities that comprise the patient's role repertoire are perhaps the single best correlation of overall mental health and resiliency. The more playful a patient is, the more there is a capacity for imagination, emotional flexibility, and what Alfred Adler called "social interest."

Simply reviewing the types of playful activities is a good reminder to patients of what might be neglected in their lifestyles, as well as being a pointer to pleasurable directions to explore. For instance, talking about noncompetitive forms of play with a person who has become fixated on competitive concerns plants a seed that there are valid and acceptable alternatives. (The questions noted in Chapter 10 are also applicable in the psychotherapeutic consultation and may serve as an example of the types of issues to pursue.)

In taking the patient's history, reviewing experiences of

play produces fruitful material about parents, siblings, schoolmates, and others. Key interactions regarding play often contain the earliest and most influential experiences. Issues of shame, guilt, triumph, cruelty, showing off, the feelings of mastery or competence, cheating, perfectionism, and many others may be addressed in such a discussion. Early events relevant to sexuality and aggression are also remembered more vividly when accessed through an exploration of the patient's history of play.

Most important in terms of catalyzing healing forces, positive experiences are rekindled in the memory when early forms of play are reviewed. As patients remember their clubhouses, forts, and hideouts, their eyes light up as they talk about the roles they played, inspired by their favorite heroes and villains on television, radio, or in the comics. Moreover, in remembering their friends, they may be helped to internalize the good feelings and validate the good parts of themselves that were evoked in their pleasant childhood pastimes.

In talking about imaginatively playful activities, there are often genuinely interesting moments for the therapist to reflect feelings of enjoyment. Patients are quite sensitive to this shift from feeling accepted to feeling enjoyed, and seeing the twinkle in a therapist's eyes strengthens the working relationship even more. A focus on material such as this in therapy helps patients restore their sense of self-esteem through knowing they can give pleasure simply by being themselves. Because discussing past and present forms of recreation often involves relatively healthy and successful aspects of the patient's personality, it tends to shift the therapist-patient relationship toward a feeling of greater equality. At least for a while, in considering the roles of play, there is a freedom from the fixed elements of the sick role. This also reduces some of the transference and resistances inherent in any helping relationship, which in turn strengthens the therapeutic alliance.

The place of play in therapy offers an ongoing acknowledgment that the therapist is an advocate of the inner child of the patient, which sustains motivation and rapport. Adjustment, responsibility, and social acceptability are obvious goals, but without the additional goals of developing creativity and having fun, the others tend to be perceived as associated with all the authority figures of the past. There's a greater sense of nurturance when the therapist and patient together reaffirm the desirability of a pleasurable solution.

Expanding the Playful Role Repertoire

One part of a total program of holistic therapy is the development of a variety of challenging, exciting, and pleasant activities that suit the patient's individuality. Patients often need to be encouraged to engage in an ongoing process of shopping and testing various recreational forms and groups. As mentioned earlier, people with emotional difficulties often need to address the specific problems in their lives, and at the same time to strengthen the other facets of their overall mental health. The two elements can work together, in the same way that treatment using surgery also requires the components of good nutrition, exercise, and other general hygienic measures in order to effect a full recovery. Similarly, the verbal psychotherapy sessions can benefit from the support, courage, and material generated for the patient in creative arts experiences. The following list indicates some of the therapeutic programs and general directions that may facilitate the patient's exploration:

Drama Therapy, involving a wide variety of exercises

Poetry, dance, art, music, and other expressive therapies

New Games and other forms of recreational therapy

Biofeedback, meditation, body/movement approaches

Guided fantasy, Ericksonian Hypnosis, Gestalt Therapy

Psychodrama, sociodrama, and role-playing in group settings

The Art of Play and creative dramatics based on imaginary characters

These may be modified, applied, and integrated into a variety of situations:

Alcohol and drug-abuse rehabilitation programs

Intermediate or long-term psychiatric facilities, including residential treatment centers and day-care outpatient clinics

Rehabilitation programs for developmental disabilities, physical handicaps, senior citizen centers, and nursing homes

The creative arts therapies provide patients with an opportunity to experience their own active expressiveness, and this then serves as a model for ways of dealing with their psychological and social problems. Whether patients are playing a role in enactments dealing with the real events in their lives (i.e., psychodrama) or in those using more imaginary characters and situations (i.e., drama therapy or the Art of Play), they are challenged to enter into encounters with the other players. The repeated experience of making interpersonal decisions in these settings increases the patients' recognition of an ability to make some choices about their behavior in their primary relationships in life.

This is especially helpful for people who have a tendency to experience themselves as helpless victims of circumstance, such as those whose behavior includes anorexia nervosa, alcoholism, or depression.[2] In a supportive group context of play, an inherent message is conveyed that it's appropriate and effective to ask for help and make use of the nurturing behaviors of others, which in turn often becomes a powerful corrective experience.[3]

Play and Addiction

A generation ago, the most commonly described emotional problem was the "neurosis," a behavioral complex usually arising out of conflicts between impulses and conscience. Today the most common problems involve a relative lack of conscience, or at least a weakened sense of the ability to take responsibility for living a well-balance life. Many people today live as if they were mildly addicted to certain habitual roles or behaviors.[4] The point is that the complaints and problems are more like addictions than neuroses. The essential dynamic of addiction involves a narrowing of the role repertoire and a fixation on certain familiar sources of satisfaction. Because there is a concurrent loss of faith which views other sources of gratification as ineffective, the fixation is self-perpetuating and resists correction, even in the face of self-defeating experiences. Put quite simply, addiction is the continuation of a behavior even when there have been repeated negative consequences.

In this sense, almost any area of human behavior can become not only a fixation, but even a psychological addiction. When examining the histories of people with these kinds of role imbalances, many of them simply don't know how else to have fun. Furthermore, it's most difficult to treat them unless the issue of another payoff can be successfully addressed. Consider the following list from this point of view:

alcohol	tobacco	sex	money
health	food	drugs	television
pets	decorating	cars	danger
fashion	news	recognition	gambling
power	work	dieting	romance
religion	children	sports	computers
gossip	crime	jogging	

Play and the Demystification of Psychology

When the therapist and patient share the same language, relatively free from jargon, then there is a mutual understanding of the nature of the problem and the overall treatment plan. This enhances the patient's sense of mastery, self-esteem, and responsibility as a co-creator of the process. The therapist, in turn, becomes more of a teacher and consultant, which reduces some of the aura of mystery which is actually more intimidating than helpful in the majority of cases. The power of the therapist doesn't come from hidden knowledge, but rather from a capacity for courageous, authentic engagement with the patient in a search for alternatives.

As mentioned in the previous chapter, talking about social and psychological phenomena in terms of roles offers an excellent, simplified language for working with group and personal experiences. Our theory of role dynamics which includes the importance of play, imagination, and spontaneity, presents how the role-playing in dramatic enactment helps people to begin to understand the dynamics of the roles played in real life. In addition, this approach emphasizes the patients' abilities creatively to modify and develop their roles, and so leads to the introduction of concepts such as improvisation, strategy, skills, negotiation, redefinition, and other process-oriented forms of mature and responsible adaptation.

Play as Metaphor

Language itself can become an instrument of mental flexibility, and the use of metaphors and poetic images which are encouraged in play then helps patients build a selection of concepts with which to think about themselves and their world. Often the imagery generated in fantasy or artistic activities can serve as important bridges to more healing experiences.

In many emotional problems or types of mental illness, the patients may be thought of as having become demoralized or having lost their spirit and vitality. Along with being burdened with worries or fears, there is also a sense of a corresponding loss of access to the sources of personal power in the forms of helpful resources, initiative, and faith. In many cultures not dominated by the Western tradition of medical or psychotherapeutic practices, the local healing approaches respond to both of these levels of illness: the intrusion of foreign influences (or "spirits") and the loss of the person's soul-power. Their healing practices thus include a combination of exorcism and reconnection of the patient with the myth, tribe, or other sources of personal healing.[5]

In modern Western psychotherapy, the equivalent of the belief that illness is caused by the intrusion of foreign spirits is the concept of either microorganisms or internalized images of parental figures. Our therapies, therefore, are aimed at freeing the person from the germs in the first case, or the unrealistic influences of the intrusive spirits of the patient's childhood. However, the healing process, if it is to be as successful as that of more "primitive" cultures, needs to consider how to help those who are demoralized to reclaim their natural heritage of personal power.[6]

One practical approach is available in improvisational drama because it helps patients to rediscover their own sources of imagery and spontaneity, and to receive validation in the process. Finding a song to sing or whistle in times of stress can be the equivalent of the shamanistic practice of finding a "power song." Developing images to express aspirations is another way to utilize the power of metaphor as a support for identity. It's similar to developing an internalized "cheering section" to express individuality and effectiveness which can be accessed in times of stress.[7]

The Art of Play may be used as an activity in treatment programs to augment psychotherapy and rehabilitation. The techniques associated with psychodrama and character development can facilitate other forms such as play therapy, group therapy, family therapy, etc.[8] Imaginative enactment offers a vehicle for broadening patients' role repertoires and for strengthening their sense of mastery and of being creators of their own lives. Other benefits include the learning of interpersonal skills and the language of role dynamics. Finally, validating pleasurable enjoyment as an important dimension of life can shift the tone and direction of therapy from narrow problem solving to holistic healing and ongoing growth and development.

Chapter 15

THE SPIRIT OF PLAY

The essence of spontaneity involves a freedom from the pressures and maneuvers that generate the inhibitions to play discussed in the previous three chapters. Indeed, playfulness is a celebration of freedom and its utilization for the production of aesthetic experience. Play partakes of a creative process which suffuses the universe and, as such, has metaphysical and spiritual qualities. These are reflected on an individual level, in the phenomenon of individuality itself; on a psychic level, in the multidimensional nature of mind; and on a cosmic level, in the ubiquitous processes of evolution.

In addition to the physical dimensions of time, space, energy, and matter, there are also psychic dimensions of relationship and aesthetics. These latter facets of reality describe the richness of the complexity and the spectrum of mind or feeling in nature. The process philosophy of Whitehead, Hartshorne, and others describes the inextricable quality of experience as part of the events which constitute the present moment.[1] The creative experience from this point of view has its own value, the value of celebration.

As Abraham Joshua Heschel[2] put it:

To celebrate is to contemplate the singularity of the moment and to enhance the singularity of the self. What was will not be again. The man of our time is losing the power of celebration. Instead of celebrating, he seeks to be amused or entertained. Celebration is an active state, an act of expressing reverence or appreciation. To be entertained is a passive state—it is to receive pleasure afforded by an amusing act or spectacle. Celebration is a confrontation, giving attention to the transcendent meaning of one's actions. (p. 115)

The significance and value of play in today's world lies also beyond the practical and social benefits, and includes deeper philosophical considerations. These have relevance in their applicability to most people's lives, for a vision of meaning in recreational experiences helps to balance overly materialistic tendencies in popular culture.

Play and Individuality

We'll begin by noting that play enhances your individuality, and this is important, because the creativity that only you can bring to the moment adds to that creativity which is the universe. There is individuality throughout nature, and in even the most minute components. This is supported by the fact that science has found incredible complexity, even at the atomic level of existence. Electrons, for example, move around the nuclei of atoms trillions of times every second, and they vibrate in "spheres" or dumbbell-shaped regions of probable locations. Because of this, every atom can be different from every other atom!

A cell, composed of trillions of atoms, can likewise be recognized as necessarily unique by virtue of its complexity. Photographs taken by the electron microscope reveal patterns of membranes in the surface of cells as complex as fingerprints. Moreover, every particle in existence varies from moment to moment and from interaction to interaction. Whitehead tried to help us change our habits of thinking in terms of separate, seemingly fixed "things" by emphasizing the actual nature of existence as process, events, and constant creative change.

If individuality is a universal phenomenon, this is a fact which probably has significance. (At least that sophisticated form of play called philosophy aims at deriving meaning from facts.) Regarding individuality's implications for human life, its celebration through play may be a way to encourage us to honor the reality of each person's uniqueness. Your individuality is not only a dynamically functioning physical assemblage of some 60 trillion cells, but it is also an incredible blend of psychosocial components.[3] Your various interests, the particulars of the imagery and music to which you resonate, your miscellaneous temperamental inclinations, strengths, weaknesses, and the many factors that contribute to your personal history, all combine to create a truly unique being. The *you* of this moment is the only you that ever was and ever will be, and your individuality offers a potential for a kind of creativity that has value because of its uniqueness.

This creativity deserves to be expressed as much as possible, within the reasonable boundaries of necessity and social harmony. Since your official roles (as family member, worker, citizen, and such) represent only a fraction of your potential range of creative possibilities, imaginative play offers a vehicle for your exploration of many other roles and ways of being.

Dimensions of the Psyche

Another deeper meaning of play involves the significance of the richness and elusive changeability of the mind. Play functions as a vehicle for practicing something akin to an active form of meditation because it freely allows the expression of intuitive and spontaneous elements, imagery, and emotion, as well as reason. It is a way to integrate the richness of the subjective realms with the infinite varieties of interpersonal and objective experience.

Discovering the essential qualities of mental playfulness is an esoteric endeavor, in that it seeks to find subtle, almost hidden patterns of meaning and relationship in a highly complex group of phenomena. In this sense, esoteric activities encompass the processes of making theoretical constructs in many fields of study—linguistics, anthropology, communications theory, natural history, subatomic physics, astronomy, biology, etc. Psychology, too, is an esoteric discipline in its attempt to clarify the workings of that most elusive phenomenon of all, consciousness itself. This is a challenge, because the nature of mind includes the very real and pervasive activity of self-deception. (The elucidation of many of the mechanisms of self-deception is the special contribution of the dynamic depth-psychologies, especially psychoanalysis and its derivatives.)

In its broadest sense, psychoanalysis has pursued the quest for understanding beyond the therapeutic context of the understanding and treating of mental illness, to include investigations into normal and even optimal functioning. A psychodynamic approach can lend depth to the study of history, comparative religion, sociology, literature, and the other humanities. Meditation, spontaneity, and many activities can engage the nonrational dimensions and can integrate them with the whole self in the service of creativity.[4] Thus, what psychoanalysis has discovered is the pervasiveness of mental phenomena which not only resist definition, but actively defy it, flout it, and subtly celebrate the poetry of the wisdom and beauty embedded in transrational states of consciousness.

The vehicle of dramatic play offers a method for bringing consciousness and social validation to the forces of imagery. Among other things, play in the adult becomes free exploratory inquiry, and allows an experimentation with the desires of the flesh and heart, sublimating them into constructive expressions, yet retaining their vibrancy and excitement.

Play as Part of Evolution

Scientific evidence about the evolution of stars, planets, and life has profoundly altered the nature of philosophy in the last century. It has become apparent that the evolutionary process is as universal a phenomenon as individuality, and thus must also be woven into our growing scheme of the meaning of life. Even if there are myriads of intelligent life forms on other worlds, human beings are nevertheless unique in the way reality is created and experienced. Evolution is a form of complexification, as if the universe is playing at finding out how many ecological niches it can live in and at the same time express some new facet of aesthetic possibility.

To understand how play serves this goal, note that evolution involves differentiation, as each species develops specialized ways to adapt, which involves increasing differentiation of cells, organs, and types within a species. This is more than simply a matter of physical diversification; it demands increasingly complex ways to exchange information within the organism and with other organisms. Thus, as species evolve, there's generally an increase in the amount and variety of forms of information exchanged within each body and with the other living creatures in the environment. Sexuality was one of the first natural methods for exchanging information—in that case, information of a genetic nature.

Yet the evolution of nervous tissue, hormones, and pheromones soon increased the numbers of types of communication, both chemical and electrochemical. Not long afterwards, many other forms evolved, using the media of sounds, pressure, heat, color, gravity, light, and other barely detectable subtleties. Issues of social communication, the complex patterns of symbiosis, territoriality, mating, and group behavior all reflected forms of exchanging information.

As humanity evolved, this process took a quantum leap, because language allows for imagination and the birth of culture. The opposable thumb and upright posture needed a capacity for organization (through communication) if a toolmaker would ever be able to progress. The complexification of culture led to new forms of consciousness.[5] Yet the rate of change in culture still depended, for the most part, on passing along the beliefs of the elders.[6] Certainly, communications over any distance tended to lack the capacity for rapid feedback and adjustments. When letters were superseded by the use of the telephone, people could talk back and forth in order to clear up any misunderstandings immediately.

The social distance between teacher and student, doctor and patient, ruler and subject also was great enough in the past so that most communications were more *directive* (i.e., from the superior in status to the inferior), rather than *mutual* in character. In the last century, however, this social distance has been altered so that the processes of therapy, education, child rearing, and management are increasingly democratic. Such transformed relationships need effective skills of two-way communications. That's where sociodramatic play comes in; it promises to be a vehicle for practice in increasing the capacity of individuals to interact constructively with others in their social networks.

As a form of multilevelled, high-feedback interaction, sociodramatic play acts to increase the fluid exchange of important interpersonal information. As our culture becomes more complex and intense, we need to communicate with more emotional warmth and sensitivity, integrating social needs along with informational content.[7]

Play, as discussed in the earlier chapters, facilitates a more sophisticated form of communication, which integrates many levels of meaning. This allows for a better understanding of the many frames of reference involved in any complex situation. It also is an early channel of rapid and fluid communicative feedback. Furthermore, it operates as a natural and enjoyable way for the learning of the component skills that are most appropriate for dealing with our changing and holistic world.

What has been described is a process of evolution, not only of the biosphere, but also for the sum total of consciousness and events of informational exchange—what the scientist-philosophter Teilhard de Chardin called "the noosphere".[8] This growth has been accelerating at a staggering rate, a geometrical expansion. If you could picture the surface of this planet with every exchange of information being a little laser pulse of light; if you could see its growth over the last thousand years using time-lapse photography; if all else could be left dark; and if you could view it from a hundred thousand miles away in space, it might look a little like some fabulously growing, living organism—perhaps an enormously magnified "cell" or a sphere-shaped "embryo" in active development!

The point is that in our present state of accelerating change, an evolutionary perspective is a useful approach. Indeed, the very concept of evolution, as it has become widely accepted, has been itself an evolutionary step in our cultural progress. From this perspective, it's useful to look at some of the trends that are operating in contemporary society. It is our hope that as we all better understand the processes, there will be a concomitant development of skills to guide the society in constructive directions.

Creativity and the Spirit

Cultures create channels for expression, even as they structure other institutions for repression. The need for freedom, however, is irrepressible, and in American society one way it finds expression is through the arts. A playful attitude is an essential component of aesthetic creativity. These activities flourish most fully when they are free from excessive utilitarian concerns.[9] By reintroducing the central theme of play for everyone (and not just for the talented specialists), there is a renewed emphasis on the experience of the creative act itself, rather than what has become an overvaluing of the finished product.

It is in the exercise of an almost meditative surrender to nondirective thought that the Muses of inspiration emerge, in their own time. This creativity finds outlets in science and research of all kinds, and not just in the arts. Yet there are excellent metaphors for the kinds of freedom of imagination in play that may be discovered in the making of music, dance, poetry, and art. All of these can express the essence of spontaneity and the spirit of play.

There is play even in philosophy and theology. Humanity has used imagination above all to conceptualize its own meaning. For example, a major sect of Christianity in the second and third centuries A.D. integrated the creative dimension into the very essence of their spiritual practice.

As Elaine Pagels[10] writes:

> Like circles of artists today, Gnostics considered original creative invention to be the mark of anyone who becomes spiritually alive. Each one, like students of a painter or writer, expected to express his own perceptions by revising and transforming what he was taught. Whoever merely repeated his teacher's words was considered immature (or 'uninitiated') . . . (p. 22)
> . . . The Gnostic Christians assumed that they had gone far beyond the Apostles' original teaching. Just as many people today assume that the most recent experiments in science or psychology will surpass earlier ones, so the Gnostics anticipated that the present and future would yield a continued increase in knowledge. (p. 25)

In the last few hundred years, philosophy and more liberal forms of theology have become more free, with a resulting flow of new, fresh ideas. More recently, many highly respected theologians and professionals in related fields of religious studies have written about the inclusion of playfulness in spiritual experience, especially the idea that there seems to be a component of "divine play" in the workings of the universe. This had been stated in other religious traditions for centuries, especially by the Hindus (in their concept of *leela*), and also by mystics and sages of Western and other Eastern cultures. (See additional references for this chapter.)

Co-Creativity and Mind Expansion

As ecological and crosscultural awareness grows, it's becoming more plausible and respectable to identify not simply with a local group, tribe, religion, or nation—nor even be limited to the human species—but to extend a sense of compassion, concern, and allegiance to include all life on this planet. Along with the growing power to destroy the world is a growing global consciousness that recognizes the interdependence and potential for the human species to learn the wisdom of becoming the caretakers. This requiries the development of a philosophy of co-creativity, a view of life that redefines the function of humanity as closer to that of cells within a great organism. The process philosophy of Whitehead and Hartshorne also advocates this theory.

The work of Teilhard de Chardin goes on to suggest some implications of this co-creative view of human nature. In his view, the most effective functioning would include a balanced mixture of individuation, cooperation, and attunement to the wholeness of things. As conscious creatures, this mode of attunement may well involve the capacity for imaginative empathy and emotional concern for the other forms of life in the world. In addition to a straightforward commitment to learn through knowledge and reason about the other components of this wholeness of which humans are a part, there is a learning that relates by using feelings and intuition. This is where role-playing becomes highly relevant.

Through exercising imagination about other people and things, through wondering what it's like to be, to experience from another's point of view, you extend your consciousness into an expanding sphere of participation. As mentioned in Chapters 1, 4 and 12, this includes many dimensions of experience—other cultures, various life forms, even inanimate forces in nature. The integration of science fiction and fantasy into the mainstream of modern literature has made it easier to engage in free flights of the mind. Thus, role-playing may be as useful a vehicle in a holistic quest for enlightenment as meditation. Indeed, imaginative and emphathic contemplation may reflect the West's active, social, and progress-oriented approach, which balances with the traditional values implicit in many of the beliefs of the East.

The Essence of Freedom

The theme of essential freedom has been a key concept throughout this chapter because it is one of the fundamental archetypal issues. The need in human beings for a deep experience of freedom must not be underestimated. Play offers an approach to this experience. As such, play must itself become free of any need to justify itself as therapy, education, personal development, art, or anything else constructive. In a way, it serves all these functions, as well as embodying some of the major implications of research in applied social psychology, child development, sociobiology, and contemporary spirituality. Furthermore, it essentially exists outside of any categorization.

Play should be recognized as an important, existentially valid human activity. What's more, it is a state of mind before it ever manifests into an activity. In play you don't need to be creative or spontaneous; you don't have to do it well; you don't have to know what or why you're doing something; and you can do "nothing."

The reclamation of childlike innocence is an act of engaging in a process suggested by many great spiritual teachers. The idea of "becoming like little children" is not a matter of following hidden rules of reward and punishment, but rather refers to a psychospiritual involvement in attuning to the essence of the transformative process. As adults reenter the realm of dramatic play through the use of spontaneity and imagination, there is a renewed participation in the wholeness of the planet and the universe. In closing, here is a quote by the early nineteenth century poet, Friedrich Schiller, which states our message quite simply:[11]

> Man only plays when he is in the fullest sense of the word a human being; and he is only fully a human being when he plays.

Chapter 16

THE FUTURE OF PLAY

The future of play lies in its being a part of a great socio-cultural leap, the integration of civilized life on this planet. If humans are fortunate and creative enough to resolve the political and ecological crises, the natural tendencies toward achieving wholeness may bring about a new level of functioning as a species. In the last century, the recognition of interdependence has become a major part of most people's awareness. It's an inevitable accompaniment of the growth of technology, because with the help of global telecommunications, people know far more about each other. Additionally, the means to travel among many countries has created a vast sense of interconnectedness. The natural human inclinations for curiosity, the desire for interesting ideas, exotic art forms and foods, romance and travel have led to a pressure for trade, exchange of philosophical and scientific theories, and other forms of cultural intercourse.

Play allows people to practice the art of encounter in a pleasant and safe context. It is a way to practice opening the mind and heart in preparation for the real meetings with others, whether they be family, international acquaintances, or perhaps even, someday, encounters with extraterrestrials.

Meeting different kinds of people from a playful stance can become an authentic interchange, rather than one in which the different sides take a superior, patronizing, or paranoid attitude.

Not only do individuals and cultures interact and generate new syntheses—technologies do also. For example, as cinema and radio developed, the idea of bringing them together was inevitable, and television was the result. A similar synthesis is being proposed in this book, the integrating of methods derived from the fields of psychotherapy, with approaches that are usually reserved for the fields of recreation and the arts.

As our culture is transforming into a new age of technology, life-style, and consciousness, the roles of both creativity and recreation require reevaluation. The Art of Play represents a hybrid of these two areas, and as much, it becomes a dynamic new resource on its own. Advances in education, psychotherapy, and group dynamics should also be considered as valuable tools in helping to forge paths into the future. Bringing together group dynamics and imaginative enactment results in a new method for developing a wide variety of skills, increasing social involvement (thereby combating alienation), and enhancing motivation (because it's fun). The Art of Play may also be considered an example of what Marshall McLuhan described:[1]

> The hybrid or meeting of two media is a moment of truth and revelation from which new form is born . . . a moment of freedom and release from the ordinary trance and numbness imposed by (the separate media) on our senses . . . The crossings of media release great force . . . (p.55)

The Social Dimension

Sociodramatic play offers an experience that balances the tendencies towards overinvolvement with the self by integrating both individuality and group process. It actively uses a major aspect of human social behavior which has received relatively little attention: the phenomenon of liking and being liked, and its function as a mediator of playful, voluntary, "unofficial" social roles. Interactions in the social dimension of liking and being liked have a different quality from—and yet interpenetrate—contractual and "official" roles (as in family, work, church, schools, or politics), and also informal roles of daily, almost anonymous, "superficial" encounters. *Liking* is a major part of the binding force in a dynamic society. The associated network of unofficial roles based on personal preferences is one of the most vigorous and interesting aspects of American culture.[2] It reflects the freedom to choose based on preferences, and it is the investigation of this informal social structure that was one of Moreno's chief interests through his method of sociometry.[3] (For further discussion of sociometry see Chapter 13.) Liking is a relatively non-self-conscious and nonrational phenomenon; it is the freedom to utilize these intuitive preferences, a freedom that is exercised in the process of play, which allows for even more freedom in the larger social structure. The goal, in other words, is to foster more friendships to counteract the alienation in society. Dinah M. Craik[4] put it:

> Oh, the comfort, the inexpressible comfort
> Of feeling safe with a person.
> Having neither to weigh thoughts,
> Nor measure words, but pouring them
> All right out—just as they are—
> Chaff and grain together—
> Certain that a faithful hand will
> Take and sift them—
> Keep what is worth keeping—
> And with the breath of kindness,
> Blow the rest away.

The conscious practice and nurturance of the unofficial roles in our culture, such as the recreational applications of imaginative play, will, over time, affect other more official roles and social institutions. People who have learned how to have and value fun will likewise begin to redefine and modify their roles at work and home in order to have more fun. At a deeper level, this means our social structures will be helped to become more humane, flexible, and responsive to individual needs. Pleasurable activities existing within the free market will exert a gentle competitive pressure on the "serious" organizational systems in order to attract participation by the population. A future result could be that instead of the individual being pressured to adjust to society, both individual and societal needs might be balanced by co-creating the necessary systems.

The Nostalgia for Play

Viewing contemporary trends from the viewpoint of depth psychology, there are many kinds of evidence suggesting that there is a widespread hunger for the reintegration of significant aspects of childhood. The romantic vision has been elaborated into science fiction, and from there into a resurgence of interest in fantasy. In the last few decades, the realms of magic, dragons, wizards, elves, goblins, monsters, rainbow enchantments, and the like have become very popular. Stimulated by the popular media, these forms have attempted to fulfill a need for personal expression through imagination.

The big business of children's toys and literature is supported by parents' choices and reveals their desires to recreate vicariously certain aspects of their own childhoods. Songs with themes about innocence and magical feelings probably rank second to romantic preoccupations, and even this popular fixation on sexual/romantic attachment is not so much an expression of genital sexual drive as a need for being liked and belonging. Adults as well as children are responsive to the newspaper comics section, Walt Disney's movies, and the Muppet Shows. People want to be "Young at Heart" and make "The Rainbow Connection." Moreover, they are hungry to become not simply spectators, but active co-creators in the realm of imagination.

A major aspect of this nostalgia is the theme of a certain

kind of freedom—the easy, relaxed, purposeless freedom that was an important part of childhood play. Christopher Robin, the little boy in A.A. Milne's Winnie-the-Pooh series, called this kind of free play "doing nothing." At the end of the two-book series, in the last chapter of *The House at Pooh Corner*, Christopher Robin takes leave of his toy bear friend, Pooh. In a poignant scene, he says he has to go off to school, and can't do "nothing" any more. Instead, he will be learning about:

> . . . people called Kings and Queens, and something called Factors, and a place called Europe, and an island in the middle of the sea where no ships came, and how you make a Suction Pump (if you wanted to), and when Knights were knighted, and what comes from Brazil.

Pooh asks Christopher Robin if he will ever do "nothing" again, and the boy replies, "Well, not so much. They don't let you."[5] Well, it's time to remedy this state of affairs. The Art of Play offers one approach that is very much like doing "nothing." You can go at your own pace, feeling free to play in whatever way you like, with whom you like, and when you like.

Options for Play

As has been noted, recent advances in technology and automation have been occurring at an accelerating rate, and this trend shows no evidence of decreasing. The personal and social effects have been channeled into more leisure-time pursuits. The need for recreational forms that are socially constructive and personally satisfying is thereby increasing. The development of creative drama activities, modified by sociodramatic methods and adapted for adults, promises to be a useful addition to the available choices. Here are some specific ideas about how sociodramatic play might be used in the future:

On a grass roots level, people could engage in informal, ongoing, clublike dramatic activities for the enjoyment of having the experience itself, rather than for performance.

There could be more imaginative playing with children, more singing, drawing, dancing, and other activities. Parents who have been played with more when they were children will grow up finding it easier to play with their own and others' children in turn.

Creative drama and role-playing have a much greater potential in the educational process. Social and psychological skills could be integrated with mastery of subject matter and vocational interests.

Classes could use more activities based on group dynamics as individualized forms of information are presented by computer-aided programmed instruction.

Celebrations in churches, synagogues, or other spiritual communities could be created with more imaginativeness to express the preferences of the specific groups.

More variations of sociodrama as theatrical forms in themselves could revitalize and personalize community experience. Jonathan Fox has created an outstanding example of this with his "Playback Theater."[6]

Radio and television shows could utilize sociodramatic ideas as the basis for modified talk shows or interviews. Instead of rehashing old themes, creative imagination could be the stimulus for new, fresh images. Guest stars or troupes of players could adapt these ideas as part of their programs.

Sociodramatic play for grownups could be one of the events at centers for the development of human potentialities. It could also be used at religious retreats or as part of programs where building group cohesion and stimulating the imagination are desired goals.

The Art of Play could become an activity at resorts or summer camps for adults with modified forms used for teenagers and children. Creative drama, New Games, and other advances in the emerging field of play all crossfertilize.

Camps, schools, and clubs could make more use of noncompetitive games, including sociodramatic play, as a balancing alternative to their programs of competitive games or performing arts.

Artists in one field could dabble more freely in other aesthetic pursuits. Thus, a dancer could experience singing for fun with a local group of artists from various fields, and a musician could explore movement. These groups would emphasize awareness rather than performance.

Spontaneity could be emphasized more in the teaching of art, music, drama, poetry, etc.

Students of the theater could engage in sociodramatic play just for fun. Of course, this will increase their flexibility and range of actions but, more important, it helps to balance the pressures toward excessive individualism, narcissism, and competitiveness which can be generated in that field.

Sociodramatic play could be actively integrated as an adjunct to programs of psychotherapy and rehabilitation. Drama therapy is already integrating psychodramatic techniques and ideas, and it, as well as psychodrama, could be used beneficially in many more settings.

Simulations and spontaneous role-playing could be used to teach interpersonal sensitivity and communications skills in schools of medicine, nursing, social work, psychology, business administration, and many others.

Sociodrama could be developed as an instrument for the clarification and resolution of political and social conflicts. Organizations, communities, and even national and international problems could be addressed with this approach.

Senior citizens could benefit from creative dramatics as a rich opportunity to share their experiences and enhance their lives. Settings for its use would be community centers, clubs and hospitals.[7–10]

Families could play, sing, and celebrate more vividly with each other. Rites of passage could be created even more meaningfully with more thought and spontaneity woven into their design.

In closing, we believe our civilization is at the threshold of yet another "Age." Just as in the Middle Ages or the Renaissance, there are powerful dynamic changes occurring which are resulting in significant shifts in human consciousness.[11, 12] The challenges of today require all of the creative resources humans can muster.[13] The Art of Play offers an attitude of mind and methods for cultivating those resources by validating much needed qualities of initiative, enthusiasm, improvisation, and inclusion. It is our hope that the ideas presented in this book will facilitate the coming transformation.

REFERENCES

Introduction:

1. Blatner, A. *Acting-in: Practical applications of psychodramatic methods*. New York: Springer, 1973. This is an excellent, simple introduction to psychodrama and it has extensive references.

2. Fleugelman, A. (Ed.). *The New Games book*. Garden City, NY: Doubleday/Dolphin, 1976. Also, *More New Games*, 1981.

3. Weinstein, M. & Goodman, J. *Playfair*. San Luis Obispo, CA: Impact Publishers, 1980.

4. DeKoven, B. *The well-played game: A players philosophy*. Garden City, NY: Doubleday/Anchor, 1978.

5. Spolin, V. *Improvisation for the theater*. Evanston, IL: Northwestern University Press, 1963. A classic.

6. Polsky, M. E. *Let's improvise*. Englewood Cliffs, NJ: Prentice-Hall, 1980.

7. Courtney, R. *Play, drama, and thought: The intellectual background to dramatic education*. London: Cassell, 1968.

8. Fleshman, B. & Fryrear, J. *The arts in therapy*. Chicago: Nelson-Hall, 1981. Excellent review of the expressive therapies.

Chapter 1: A Psychology and Philosophy of Play

1. Wallach, M. A., & Wallach, L. *Psychology's sanction for selfishness: The error of egoism in theory and therapy*. San Francisco: W.H. Freeman & Co., 1983.

2. Stern, D. *The interpersonal world of the infant*. New York: Basic Books, 1985.

3. Blatner, A. Spontaneity. Chapter 7 In *Foundations of psychodrama*. New York: Springer, in press, 1988. This is an updated complement to *Acting-in* (op. cit.).

4. Wigginton, E. *Sometimes a shining moment: The foxfire experience—Twenty years teaching in a high school classroom*. Garden City, NY: Anchor Press/Doubleday, 1985.

5. Whitehead, A. N. *Modes of thought*. New York: The Free Press, 1938.

6. Hartshorne, C. *Omnipotence and other theological mistakes*. Albany, NY: SUNY Press, 1983.

7. Teilhard de Chardin, P. *Hymn of the universe*. New York: Harper Torchbooks, 1965.

8. Wilber, K. *Eye to eye: The quest for the new paradigm*. Garden City, NY: Anchor Press/Doubleday, 1983.

9. Skutch, A. F. *Life ascending*. Austin, TX: University of Texas Press, 1986.

Chapter 2: The Pleasures of Paradox

1. Huizinga, J. *Homo ludens—a study of the play element in culture*. Boston: Beacon Press, 1955. This is a classic in the field.

2. Freud, S. The Relation of the Poet to Day-Dreaming, *Collected Papers*, Vol. 4. London, Hogarth Press, 1925, pp.172–183.

3. Sapora, A. V., & Mitchell, E. D. *The theory of play and recreation* (3rd ed.). New York: The Ronald Press, 1961.

4. Bateson, G. The Message, This is Play. In (Ed.) B. Schaffner, *Group processes: Transactions of the second conference*. New York: Josiah Macy, Jr. Foundation, 1956.

5. Fry, W., Jr. *Sweet madness—A study of humor*. Palo Alto, CA: Pacific Books, 1963.

6. Fry, W., Jr., & Allen, M. *Make 'em laugh*. Palo Alto, CA: Science and Behavioral Books, 1975.

7. Bretherton, I. Representing the social world. In (Ed.) I. Bretherton *Symbolic play: The development of social understanding*. Orlando, FL: Academic Press, 1984.

8. Moreno, J. L. Psychiatry of the twentieth century: Function of the universalia: Time, Space, Reality, and Cosmos, *Group Psychotherapy*, 1966, *19*, pp.146–158.

9. Blatner, A. The dynamics of catharsis, *Journal of Group Psychotherapy, Psychodrama, and Sociometry*, Jan. 1985, *37*, (No. 4) pp.157–166.

Chapter 3: The Benefits of Play

1. McCaslin, N. *Creative drama in the classroom*. (4th Ed.). New York: Longman, 1984, pp. 393–396.

2. Moreno, J. L. *Who shall survive?* Beacon, NY: Beacon Press (1st ed.) 1934, pp. 325–6.

3. Comstock, G. Media influences on aggression, In A. Goldstein (Ed.), *Prevention and control of aggression*. New York: Pergamom Press, 1983.

4. Blatner, A. The dynamics of catharsis, *Journal of Group Psychotherapy, Psychodrama, and Sociometry*, Jan. 1985, *37* (No. 4) pp. 157–166.

5. Moyers, B. The meaning of creativity, *Smithsonian*, January, 1982, *12* (10) pp. 64–75.

6. Torrance, E. P. *The search for satori and creativity*. Buffalo, NY: Creative Education Foundation, 1979.

7. Luthe, W. *Creativity mobilization technique*. New York: Grune & Stratton, 1976.

8. Montagu, A. *Growing Young*. New York: McGraw-Hill, 1981.

Further References on Creativity

Arasteh, A.R., & Arasteh, J.D. *Creativity in human development*. Cambridge, MA: Schenkman, 1976.

Arieti, S. *Creativity: The magic synthesis*. New York: Basic Books, 1976.

Koestler, A. *The act of creation*. London: Hutchinson & Co., 1976.
May, R. *The courage to create*. New York: Norton, 1975.
Mooney, R. & Razik, T.A. (Eds). *Explorations in creativity*. New York: Harper & Row, 1967.
Rosner, S. & Abt, L. (Eds.), *The creative experience*. New York: Grossman, 1970, pp. 379–399, reviewing the literature.
Rothenberg, A., & Hausman, C. R. (Eds.). *The creativity question*. Durham, NC: Duke University Press, 1976.
Vandenberg, B. Play, problem-solving, and creativity. In K. Rubin, Ed. *Children's play*. San Francisco: Jossey-Bass, 1980, pp. 49–68.

Chapter 4: An Orientation to the Art of Play

1. Bandler, R., & Grinder, J. *Frogs into princes: Neuro-linguistic programming*. Moab, UT: Real People Press, 1979.

Chapter 6: Fundamentals of Enactment

1. Samples, B. *The metaphoric mind: A celebration of creative consciousness*. Reading, MA: Addison-Wesley, 1976.

2. Hampden-Turner, C. *Maps of the mind*. New York: MacMillan, 1981.

3. Mason, L. J. *Guide to stress reduction*. Culver City, CA: Peace Press, 1980.

4. Doyle, A. C. *The Sherlock Holmes pocket book*. New York: Pocket Books, 1941, pp. 353–355.

5. Stevens, J. O. *Awareness: Exploring, experimenting, experiencing*. New York: Bantam, 1973.

Chapter 7: Elaborating Roles

1. Schultz, D. P. *A history of modern psychology*. New York: Academic Press, 1969, p. 111.

2. Hayakawa, S. I. *Language in thought and action*. New York: Harcourt, Brace, & Co., 1949, p. 96.

3. Krupar, K. R. *Communication games: A participant's manual*. New York: The Free Press, 1973, pp. 23–26.

Chapter 8: Using Dramatic Techniques

1. Leveton, E. *Psychodrama for the timid clinician*. New York: Springer, 1977.

Further References on Techniques for Dramatic Play

Cranston, J. *Dramatic imagination*. Arcata, CA: Interface Press, 1975.

Hodgson, J. & Richards, E. *Improvisation*. New York: Grove Press, 1966.

Hooper, C., et. al. *Awareness games (Die Spielende Gruppe)*. New York: St. Martin's Press, 1974.

Johnstone, K. *Impro: Improvisation and the theater*. New York: Theater Arts Books, 1979.

Kelly, E. Y. *The magic if: Stanislavsky for children*. Baltimore, MD: National Education Press, 1973.

Moreno, Z. *A survey of psychodramatic techniques*. Beacon, NY: Beacon House, 1975.

Quell, B. *Get those people moving: A handbook of creative dramatics*. Albany, NY: Albany City Arts Office, 1981.

Remocker, A. J. & Storch, E. T. *Action speaks louder: A handbook of nonverbal group techniques*. New York: Churchill-Livingston, 1979.

Chapter 9: Integrating Other Dimensions of Spontaneity

1. Grenough, M. Sing it! *Journal of Group Psychotherapy, Psychodrama, and Sociometry, 1983, 36* (2) pp. 69–77.

2. Newman, F. R. *Mouth sounds*. New York: Workman, 1980. A hilarious book.

3. J.M. Belis, Laughter, play and song. In J. Cassius, Ed. *Horizons in Bioenergetics*. Memphis, TN: Promethean Publications, 1980.

4. Bartenieff, I. *Body Movement: Coping with the environment*. New York: Gordon & Breach Science Publishers, 1980).

5. *Research in dance: problems and possibilities—A symposium*. New York: Postgraduate Center for Mental Health, 1970.

6. Kellogg, R. *Analyzing children's art*. Palo Alto, CA: National Press Books, 1970.

7. Wilson, M. & B. *Teaching children to draw*. Englewood Cliffs, NJ: Prentice-Hall, 1982.

8. Arguelles, J. & M. *Mandala*, Berkeley, CA: Shambala, 1972.

9. Ward, C. H. Kilroy was here. *Psychoanalytic Quarterly*, 1962, *31*: 80.

10. Brain, R. *The decorated body*. New York: Harper & Row, 1979.

11. Marsh, S. III, Amarillo, Texas.

Chapter 10: The Inhibition of Play

1. Moody, R., Jr. *Laugh after laugh: The healing power of humor*. Jacksonville, FL: Headwaters Press, 1978, p.119.

2. Strecker, E. A., & Appel, K. A. *Discovering ourselves*. New York: Macmillan, 1962, pp.183–5.

3. Bettelheim, B. *Freud and man's soul*. New York: Alfred A. Knopf, 1983, pp.20–30.

4. Shostrom, E. L. *Man, the manipulator*. Nashville, TN: Abington Press, 1967.

5. Pogrebin, L. C. *Family politics*. New York: McGraw-Hill, 1983.

6. Kaplan, H. I. & Sadock, B. *Sensitivity through encounter and marathon*. New York: E. P. Dutton, 1972. Actually, Moreno coined the term "acting-out"; psychoanalysis co-opted it, but they changed his meaning completely (p.12).

7. Blatner, H. A. Comments on some commonly held reservations about psychodrama, *Group Psychotherapy*, 1968, *21*(No.1), pp.20–25.

8. Orlick, T. *Winning through cooperation*. Washington, DC: Acropolis Books, 1978.

9. Nesbitt, J. *Megatrends*. New York: Warner Books, 1982.

10. Nierenberg, G. I. *Fundamentals of negotiating*. New York: Hawthorne/Dutton, 1973.

Chapter 11: Reality and Fantasy

1. Horowitz, M. *States of mind*. New York: Plenum, 1979.

2. Samples, R. *The metaphoric mind*. Boston: Addison-Wesley, 1976.

3. Wharf, B. L. An American Indian model of the universe. In D. Tedlock, Ed. *Teachings from the earth*. New York: Liveright, 1975.

4. Perrot, L. Doubling as an Existential-Phenomenological viewpoint, *Group Psychotherapy and Psychodrama*, 1975, *28*, pp. 66–69.

5. Sax, S., & Hollander, S. *Reality games: Games people ought to play*. New York: Popular Library, 1972.

6. Watkins, M. *Invisible guests: The development of imaginal dialogue*. Hillsdale, N.J.: The Analytic Press/L. Erlbaum, 1986.

7. Pruyser, P. W. *The play of the imagination: Toward a psychoanalysis of culture*. New York: International Universities Press, 1983.

Chapter 12: Play's Vulnerability to Judgment

1. Kellogg, R. *Analyzing children's art*. Palo Alto, CA: National Press Books, 1970.

2. Wilson, M. & B. *Teaching children to draw*. Englewood Cliffs, N.J.: Prentice-Hall, 1982.

3. Orlick, T. & Botterill, C. *Every kid can win*. Chicago, IL: Nelson-Hall, 1975.

4. Callois, R. *Man, play and games*. New York: The Free Press of Glencoe, 1961, pp. 43–55.

5. Rubin, H. *Competing*. New York: Lippincott & Crowell, 1980.

6. Friedman, M. & Rosenman, R. *Type A behavior and your heart*. Greenwich, CT: Fawcett Publications, 1975.

7. Robertson, W. *Free to act: How to star in your own life*. New York: Putnam, 1978.

Further References on Competition

Orlick, T. *The second co-operative sports and games book*. New York: Pantheon Books, 1978.

--*ibid*. *Winning through co-operation*. Washington, DC: Acropolis Books, 1978.

Sobel, J. *Everybody wins: A handbook of non-competitive games*. New York: Walker & Co. 1983.

Tutko, T. & Bruns, W. *Winning is everything and other American myths*. New York: Macmillan, 1976.

Chapter 13: Applications in Education

1. Shaftel, F. R. & Shaftel, G. *Role playing in the curriculum* (2nd ed.). Englewood Cliffs, NJ: Prentice-Hall, 1982. This scholarly and excellent resource was first published in 1967 with the title *Role playing for social values* (same publishers).

2. Fordyce, R. *Children's theater and creative dramatics: An annotated bibliography of critical works*. Boston: G.K. Hall, 1975.

3. Hale, A. E. Warm up to a sociometric exploration, *Group Psychotherapy and Psychodrama*, 1974, *27*, pp. 157–172.

4. *--ibid*. The role diagram expanded, *Group Psychotherapy and Psychodrama*, 1975, *28*, pp. 77–104.

5. Emerson, R. W. History. In *Essays*. Boston: Houghton Mifflin, 1885.

6. Pearce, J. C. *Magical child matures*. New York: Bantam, 1985, pp. 83–85.

General References: Sociodramatic Play in Education

Barnfield, G. *Creative drama in schools*. New York: Hart Publishing, 1969.

Brown, G. I. *Human teaching for human learning*. New York: Viking, 1971.

Chilver, P. *Teaching improvised drama: A handbook for secondary schools*. London: B.T. Batsford, Ltd., 1978.

Courtney, R. *Play, drama, and thought: The intellectual background to dramatic education*. London: Cassell, 1968.

Duke, C. *Creative dramatics and English teaching*. Urbana, IL: National Council of Teachers of English. 1974.

Furness, P. *Role playing in the elementary school*. New York: Hart Publishing Co., 1976.

Gray, F., & Mager, G. C. *Liberating education: Psychological learning through improvisational drama*. Berkeley, CA: McCutchan Publishing Co., 1973.

Haas, R. B. (Ed.) *Psychodrama and sociodrama in American education*. Beacon, NY: Beacon House, 1949.

Hawley, R. *Value exploration through role play*. New York: Hart Publishing Co. 1975.

Heinig, R. B., & Stillwell, L. *Creative dramatics for the classroom teacher*. Englewood Cliffs, NJ: Prentice-Hall, 1975.

Landy, R. J. *Handbook of educational drama and theater*. Westport, Conn: Greenwood Press, 1982.

McCaslin, N. (Ed.) *Children and drama*. New York: Longman, 1981.

McCaslin, N. *Creative dramatics in the classroom*. New York: David McKay Co., 1984. (The recent edition has an excellent annotated and updated bibliography.)

Pinkerton, T. *Breaking communication barriers with role play*. Atlanta, GA: John Knox Press, 1976.

Shuman, R. *Educational drama for today's schools*. Metuchen, NJ: The Scarecrow Press, 1978.

Siks, G. B. *Drama with children*. New York: Harper & Row, 1983.

Stanford, G. & Roark, A. E. *Human interaction in education*. Boston: Allyn & Bacon, 1974.

Torrance, E. P. *Encouraging creativity in children*. Dubuque, Iowa: Wm. G. Brown, Co., 1970.

Wagner, B. J. *Dorothy Heathcote: Drama as a learning medium*. Washington, DC: National Education Association of U.S., 1976.

Ward, W. *Playmaking with children*. (2nd ed.) New York: Appleton-Century-Crofts, 1957.

Way, B. *Development through drama*. London: Longman, 1967.

Chapter 14: Spontaneity, Playfulness, and Psychotherapy

1. Laing, R. D. *Knots*. New York: Pantheon Books, 1970.

2. Seligman, M. E. *Helplessness*. San Francisco: W.H. Freeman & Co., 1975.

3. Trower, P., Bryant, B. R., & Argyle, M. *Social skills and mental health*. Pittsburgh: University of Pittsburgh Press, 1978, pp. 73–95.

4. Peele, S. *Love and addiction*. New York: Taplinger, 1975.

5. Harner, M. *The way of the shaman*. New York: Bantam, 1982.

6. Torrey, E. F. *The mind game: Witch doctors and psychiatrists*. New York: Emerson Hall, 1972.

7. Storm, H. *Seven arrows*. New York: Ballantine, 1972.

8. Blatner, A., M.D. *Foundations of psychodrama*. op.cit.

Chapter 15: The Spirit of Play

1. Hartshorne, C. *Whitehead's philosophy*. Lincoln, NE: University of Nebraska Press, 1972.

2. Heschel, A. J. *Who is man?* Stanford, CA: Stanford University Press, 1965, pp. 115–118.

3. Williams, R. J. *You are extraordinary*. New York: Random House, 1967.

4. Wilber, K. *A sociable god: A brief introduction to a transcendental sociology*. New York: McGraw-Hill/New Press, 1983.

5. Jaynes, J. *The origins of consciousness in the breakdown of the bicameral mind*. Boston: Houghton-Mifflin, 1976.

6. Mead, M. *Culture and commitment*. Garden City, NY: Natural History Press/Doubleday & Co., 1970.

7. Nesbitt, J. *Megatrends*. New York: Warner Books, 1982, Chapter 3.

8. Teilhard de Chardin, P. *The future of man*. New York: Harper & Row, 1964, pp. 155–184.

9. Rader, M., & Jessup, B. *Art and human values*. Englewood Cliffs, NJ: Prentice-Hall, 1976, pp. 340–346.

10. Pagels, E. *The Gnostic Gospels* New York: Random House, 1979.

11. Schiller, F. *On the aesthetic education of man in a series of letters*, E. M. Wilkinson & L. A. Willoughby (Eds.) Oxford, England: Clarendon Press, 1967, p. 215.

References on the Spirit of Play

Barrager, P. *Spiritual understanding through creative drama*. Valley Forge, PA: Judson Press, 1981.

Cox, H. *The feast of fools*. New York: Harper/Colophon, 1969.

DeSola, C. *The spirit moves: A handbook of dance and prayer*. Washington, D.C.: The Liturgical Conference, 1977.

Johari, H. *Leela: The game of self-knowledge*. New York: Coward, McCann & Geoghegan, 1975.

Kinsley, D. R. *The divine player: A study of Krishna Leela*. Delhi, India: Motilal Banarsidass, 1979.

McLelland, J. *The clown and the crocodile*. Richmond, VA: John Knox Press, 1970.

Miller, D. L. *Gods and games: Toward a theology of play*. Cleveland, OH: World Publishers, 1970.

Moltman, J. *Theology of play*. New York: Harper & Row, 1972.

Neale, R. E. *In praise of play: Toward a psychology of religion*. New York: Harper & Row, 1969.

Perry, W. (Ed.). *A treasury of traditional wisdom*. London: George Allen & Unwin, Ltd. 1971. pp. 33–36.

Rahner, H. *Man at play*. New York: Herder & Herder, 1972.

Watts, A. *Beyond theology: The art of godmanship*. New York: Random House/Vintage, 1964. (Especially Chapter 2, entitled, "Is it serious?")

Chapter 16: The Future of Play

1. McLuhan, M. *Understanding media*. New York: McGraw-Hill Paperback, 1965, p. 55.

2. Slavin, N. *When two or more are gathered together*. New York: Farrar, Straus, & Giroux, 1976.

3. Moreno, J. L. *Who shall survive?—Foundations of sociometry*. New York: Beacon House, 1953.

4. Craik, D. M. M. Friendship In *Friendship*, compiled by R. L. Woods. Norwalk, Conn: The C.R. Gibson Company, 1969.

5. Milne, A. A. *The house at Pooh Corner*. New York: E.P. Dutton & Co., 1928), pp. 172–179. (This story had a profound influence on us; it's at the top of our recommended reading.)

6. Fox, J. Playback theater: The community sees itself. In G. Schattner & R. Courtney (Eds.). *Drama in therapy*, Vol. II, New York: Drama Book Specialists, 1981, pp. 295–308.

7. Michaels, C. Geriadrama. In *Drama in therapy*, Vol. II, op, cit., pp. 175–192.

8. Caplow-Lindner, E., Harpaz, L., & Samberg, S. *Therapeutic dance/movement—Expressive activities for older adults*. New York: Human Sciences Press, 1979.

9. Thurman, A. & Piggins, C. Drama activities with older adults. In *Expressive therapy with elders and the disabled*. New York: The Haworth Press, 1982.

10. Weisberg, N. & Wilder, R. (Eds.) *Creative arts with older adults: A sourcebook*. New York: Human Sciences Press, 1985.

11. Roszak, T. *The unfinished animal*. New York: Harper & Row, 1975.

12. Toffler, A. *The third wave*. New York: W. Morrow & Co., 1980.

13. Capra, F. *The turning point: Science, society, and the rising culture*. New York: Bantam Books, 1983.

GENERAL BIBLIOGRAPHY ON PLAY

Aldis, O. *Play fighting*. New York: Academic Press, 1975.

Alexander, F. A contribution to the theory of play, *Psychoanalytic Quarterly*, 1958, *27*:175–193.

Bach, G. R. Dramatic play therapy with adult groups. *Journal of Psychology*, 1950, *29*, 225–246.

Barrell, J. *Playgrounds of our minds*. New York: Columbia University Teachers College Press, 1980.

Bateson, G. A. A theory of play and fantasy, *Psychiatric Research Reports*, 1955, Vol. 2, pp. 39–51.

Berlyne, D. E. Laughter, humor and play. In G. Lindzey & E. Aronson (Eds.) *The handbook of social psychology*, Vol. 3. Reading, MA: Addison-Wesley, 1969.

Blatner, A. *Foundations of psychodrama: History, theory, and practice*. New York: Springer (in press) 1988. Further articles on spontaneity and the intellectual basis of the Art of Play.

Bretherton, I. (Ed.) *Symbolic play: The development of social understanding*. Orlando, FL: Academic Press, 1984.

Bro, H. H. *High play: Turning on without drugs*. New York: Coward-McCann, 1970.

Brown, C. C. & Gottfried, A. W. (Eds.) *Play interactions: The role of toys and parental involvement in children's development.* Johnson & Johnson Baby Products Co. (P.O. Box 836, Somerville, N.J. 08876. $7.00), 1985.

Bruner, J. S., Jolly, A., & Silva, K. (Eds.). *Play: Its role in development and evolution.* New York: Basic Books, 1971. (Extensive anthology of many relevant resources.)

Bruner, J. S. The nature and uses of immaturity, *American Psychologist*, 1972, 27: 687–708.

Caplan, F. & Caplan, T. *The power of play.* New York: Anchor/Doubleday & Co., 1973.

Callois, R. *Man, play and games.* New York: The Free Press of Glencoe, 1961.

Chance P. (Ed.). *Learning through play: A symposium.* New York: Johnson & Johnson Co./Gardner Press, 1979.

Cherfas, J. & Lewin, R. *Not work alone: A cross-cultural view of play.* Beverly Hills, CA: Sage Publications, 1980.

Courtney, R. *Play, drama and thought: The intellectual background to dramatic education.* London: Cassell, 1968.

Curry, N., et al. *Play: The child strives toward self-realization.* Washington, D.C.: National Association for the Education of Young Children, 1971.

Ellis, M. J. *Why people play.* Englewood Cliffs, NJ: Prentice-Hall, 1973.

Ellis, M. J. & Scholtz, G. J. L. *Activity and play of children.* Englewood Cliffs, NJ: Prentice-Hall, 1978.

Fagan, R. *Animal play behavior.* New York: Oxford University Press, 1981.

Fink, E. The ontology of play, *Philosophy Today*, Summer, 1974, Vol. 8, No. 2, pp. 147–161.

Garvey, C. *Play.* Cambridge, MA: Harvard University Press, 1977.

Hans, J. S. *The play of the world.* Amherst, MA: University of Massachusetts Press, 1981.

Harris, J. C. Play: A definition and implied interrelationships with culture and sport, *Journal of Sport Psychology*, 1980, 2 (1), 46–61.

Hartley, R. E., Frank, L. K., & Goldenson, R. M. *Understanding children's play.* New York: Columbia University Press, 1952.

Herron, R. & Sutton-Smith, B. (Eds.). *Child's play.* New York: John Wiley & Sons, 1971.

Huizinga, J. *Homo Ludens: A study of the play element in culture*. Boston: Beacon Press, 1955. A classic.

Ireland, L. *The experience of being playful in therapy and theater: A phenomenological approach*. Ph.D. dissertation, California Institute of Integral Studies, San Francisco, 1984.

Jones, R. E. *The dramatic imagination*. New York: Theater Arts Books, 1941.

Koste, V. G. *Dramatic play in childhood: Rehearsal for life*. New Orleans, LA: Anchorage Press, 1978.

Lancy, D. & Tindall, A. (Eds.) *The anthropological study of play*. Cornwall, N.Y.: Leisure Press, 1976.

Levy, J. *Play behavior*. New York: John Wiley & Sons. 1978.

Lieberman, J. N. *Playfulness: Its relationship to imagination and creativity*. New York: Academic Press, 1977.

Loizos, C. Play in mammals. In P. A. Jewell & C. Loizos. (Eds.). *Play, exploration, and territoriality in mammals*. London: Academic Press, 1966.

Lowenfeld, M. *Play in childhood*. New York: John Wiley & Sons, 1967. (Originally published in England in 1935).

Millar, S. *The psychology of play*. New York: Penguin Books, 1968.

Monaghan, T. A. *Releasing playfulness in the adult through creative drama*. New York: Columbia Teachers College, Ed.D. thesis, Dept. of Theater, 1976.

Muller-Schwarze, D. (Ed.). *Evolution of play behavior*. Stroudsburg, PA: Dowden, Hutchinson & Ross, 1978.

Peller, L. E. Libidinal phases, ego development, and play, *The Psychoanalytic study of the child*, 1954, 9: 178–198.

Piaget, J. *Play, dreams, and imitation in childhood*. New York: W.W. Norton & Co., 1962.

Piers, M. W. (Ed.), *Play and development: A symposium*. New York: W.W. Norton & Co., 1972.

Plessner, H. *Laughing and crying*. (J. Churchill & M. Grene, trans. Evanston, IL: Northwestern University Press, 1970, pp. 76–80.

Reilly, M. (Ed.). *Play as exploratory learning*. Beverly Hills, CA: Sage Publications, 1974. (Excellent review including a number of incisive chapters by the editor.)

Rubin, K. H. (Ed.) *Children's play*. New Directions for Child Development, #9. San Francisco: Jossey-Bass, 1980. This consists of a number of useful articles.

Rubin, K. H., Fein, G. G., & Vandenberg, B. Play. In P.H. Mussen (Ed.), *Handbook of Child Psychology* (4th ed.). New York: John Wiley & Sons, 1983. pp. 693–774. This is a scholarly and extensive review of the field.

Sadler, W. A., Jr. *Existence and love*. New York: Charles Scribner's Sons, 1969. pp. 216–220.

Sapora, A. V., & Mitchell, E. D. *The theory of play and recreation* (3rd ed.). New York: The Ronald Press, 1961.

Schwartzman, H. B. Works on play: A bibliography. In P. Stevens, Jr. (Ed.), *Studies in the anthropology of play*. New York: Leisure Press, 1977.

Schwartzman, H. B. *Transformations: The anthropology of children's play*. New York: Plenum Press, 1978.

Schwartzman, H. B. (Ed.). *Play and culture: 1978 Proceedings of the Association for the Anthropological Study of Play*. New York: Leisure Press, 1980.

Singer, J. *The child's world of make-believe*, New York: Academic Press, 1973.

Singer, J. & Switzer, E. *Mind play: The creative use of fantasy*. Englewood Cliffs, NJ: Prentice-Hall, 1980.

Slade, P. *The experience of spontaneity*. London: Longman Group, 1968.

Slovenko, R. & Knight, J. A. (Eds.). *Motivations in play, games, and sports*. Springfield, IL: Charles C. Thomas, 1967.

Smith, E. O. (Ed.). *Social play in primates*. New York: Academic Press, 1978.

Smith, P. K. (Ed.). *Play in animals and humans*. Oxford, England: Basil, Blackwell, 1984.

Sutton-Smith, B. (Ed.) *Play and learning*. New York: Gardner Press, 1979.

Sylva, K. Play on learning. In B. Tizard & D. Harvey (Eds.), *Biology of play*. London: Heinemann, 1977.

TAASP (The Association for the Anthropological Study of Play), Proceedings, 10 Volumes, 1976–Present. Human Kinetics Publishers, Inc., Box 5076, Champaign, IL 61820.

Tizard, B., & Harvey, D. (Eds.). *Biology of play*. London: Spastics International Medical Publications, 1977.

Vandenberg, B. Environmental and cognitive factors in social play, *Journal of Experimental Psychology*, 1981, *31*, 169–175.

Watts, A. Letting go: The art of playful living. *East West Journal*, April 1983, pp. 30–36.

Westland, C. & Knight, J. *Playing, living, learning*. State College, PA: Venture Publishing, Inc., 1982. (This interesting review, put out in cooperation with the World Leisure and Recreation Association and The International Association for the Child's Right to Play, describes a wide scope of activities and resources.)

Wilkinson, P. F. (Ed.). *In celebration of play*. New York: St. Martin's Press, 1980.

Wilshire, B. *Role playing and identity: The limits of theater as metaphor*. Bloomington, IN: Indiana University Press, 1982.

Winnicott, D. W. *Playing and reality*. New York: Basic Books, 1971.

Yawkey, T. D. & Pellegrini, A. D. (Eds.) *Child's play: Developmental and applied*. Hillsdale, NJ: Lawrence Erlbaum, Assoc., Inc., 1984. (A very nice anthology of current developments, especially regarding the place of sociodramatic play in childhood.)

Yawkey, T. D., & Pellegrini, A. D. (Eds.) *Child's play and play therapy*. Lancaster, PA: Technomic Publishing Co., 1984. (Another anthology noting applications in therapy.)

Yawkey, T. D. & Miller, T. J. The language of social play in young children. In A. D. Pellegrini & T. Yawkey (Eds.), *The development of oral and written language in social contexts*. Norwood, NJ: Ablex Publishing Corp., 1984.